PUT YOUR SELF
ON THE SHELF

Let God
Answer
Your Prayers

By Marion Clark, Intercessor

PUT YOUR SELF ON THE SHELF

Let God Answer Your Prayers

By Marion Clark, Intercessor

Published by:
Intermedia Publishing Group
P.O. Box 2825
Peoria, Arizona 85380
www.intermediapub.com

ISBN # 978-0-9820458-5-5

Printed in the United States of America by Epic Print Solutions

WARNING! WARNING! WARNING!
This Book May Be Hazardous to Your "SELF"

YOUR "SELF" HAS TO GO!
IT IS HINDERING GOD'S ANSWERS TO YOUR PRAYERS.

This book is not for spiritual sissies. If you are really serious, or maybe even desperate for answers to prayer, you're going to have to be willing to shift your focus from Self to God.

All the visual characterizations of your Self that you see named on the front cover are actually representations of your selfish desires which struggle against your spirit for control of your life. They prevent you from growing spiritually and keep you from connecting with God. Self uses your emotions to protest against everything that leads to God. Self knows that once you know God, it becomes yesterday's "liver and onions". Therefore, to protect Self's power over mind and will, it continues to strengthen an impenetrable stone wall between you and God. The only way to shatter this wall is with the truth of God's Word. God says that His Word is like fire and a hammer that breaks rock into rubble. Nothing can withstand the power of God's mighty hammer.

The challenge to change is aimed straight at the core of your Self-being. If you accept it, you will be blessed by placing God in His rightful place on the throne of your heart. This book will guide you through a journey, a process of removing your "Self" and letting God empower your motivations. Once Self is out of the way, all the lies you have believed will no longer block your communication and your relationship with God.

Yes, you really have been blocking God's answers to your

prayers. And all this time you were blaming <u>Him</u>? Does it startle you that <u>you</u>, your Self - not God - are the hang-up in receiving God's response? God wants to talk to you so He has provided a way for you to reach Him. Are you willing to do *whatever it takes* to get answers from God?

Get with it! Time's a-wastin'! Find out what you've been doing your Self's way that does not match God's way. Think of all the days, months, years you have waited without answers. Learn how to examine your heart; read and meditate on the scriptures provided; pray the focused prayers with belief and sincerity; make the out-loud declarations; learn to trust and believe that God will do what He says He will do. With the guidance of the **Holy Spirit**, you *will* succeed in breaking down the stone wall that Self built. He will help you remove your Self from blocking God's answers. Then when Self is removed, "Let 'er rip!" Receive new prayer power, new authority, new spiritual insights, a stronger relationship with God, and – at last - answers to your prayers. God is God of more than enough. He always gives you more than you ask. God is *for you*. He encourages you to succeed. The only one stopping you from victory is-- your "Self" and your lack of knowledge.

No, you don't have to struggle alone in ignorance. This guide is designed for your use as you journey through unfamiliar territory towards effective prayer. <u>If</u>, however, you are not ready to commit, you can't handle change or digging around in things about your Self that you'd rather not think about, then put the book down now! You'll be wasting your time in reading it. Make your decision **now.** If you so choose, God will see your heart and meet you on the road even as you begin your journey towards fervent effective prayer. God is in the success business! He cannot be beaten and neither can His children, including **you**.

MY WITNESS AND ENCOURAGEMENT
TO YOU

How did I come to know these things and why should you

consider what I say? I have walked through this process myself. I just wish that I could have learned sooner what I'm passing on to you. I take very seriously **Hosea 4:6** *My people are destroyed from lack of knowledge.*

My lack of knowledge was destroying my relationships and my life. I had faith, but I lacked knowledge of the Bible and I didn't know that God's Word could teach me how to pray. I had more confidence in my Self than I had in God. I thought that I could handle everything even in the midst of my mistakes. I knew *about* God. I didn't know *Him.*

There is no limit to what you can know about God and prayer once Self is on the shelf. What you don't know about prayer often keeps you from receiving what you pray for. I prayed in ignorance for loved ones for over 20 years and nothing happened until I learned that I needed to pray in God's will according to His written word not what my mind and emotions told me to pray. *Once I stopped praying intellectual, Self-ish prayers,* I began to get answers. A silken veil of peace softly slipped around me. I was no longer anxious, sleepless, filled with doubt and fear. What joy God has in store for you! Let the Holy Spirit within you be your prayer mentor. He has been, and remains my trusted prayer counselor.

Marion Clark, Intercessor

TABLE OF CONTENTS

BEGINNING YOUR JOURNEY

Why don't I get answers to my prayers? That's a tricky question because we are all at a different place in our relationship with God. Most of all, we may not understand how the Holy Spirit works within us. Without knowledge *of* and belief *in* the Holy Spirit, our prayers are operating on AAA battery power when we could have atomic power. It is the Holy Spirit who empowers our prayers and connects us with God. He teaches, leads, encourages, and sometimes even prays *for* us as He draws us nearer to God.

When Jesus ascended into heaven, He did not leave us as orphans. He asked the Father to send the Holy Spirit to live within us. If Jesus thought we needed the Holy Spirit, then I'm in agreement with <u>Him</u>. I want to receive all the power, authority, and wisdom I can get! I know that by myself, of myself, I can do nothing without God. Plug in to God, your spiritual power source. Forget your own imperfect understanding grounded in Self. Ask the Holy Spirit in you to lead you into all truth. You do have Him, you know. You received Him when you claimed Jesus as your Lord and Savior. You couldn't have done that without Him. It was the Holy Spirit that revealed Jesus, God's Son, to you in the first place. Ask the Holy Spirit to teach and to guide you as you learn more about receiving answers to prayer.

PROCESS

These following scriptures are basic to your understanding the 1... 2... 3... step process of removing the Self rocks that you have placed between you and God. Even now - right this minute - Self is blocking the prayer answers that God has already sent to you.

Step 1.   Psalm 139:23

Search me, O God, and know my heart: try me, and know my thoughts. As you read, you will <u>identify your heart attitudes</u>, motivations, and actions formed by your Self, and in your own self-interest.

1

Step 2.   Psalm139:24

And see if there be any wicked way in me, and lead me in the way everlasting. You will learn to pray according to God's will, not your own. You will also learn to pray God's word back to Him. When you learn to pray according to God's requirements, you will move from Self-focused prayers to God-focused prayers. Then the answers will come.

Step 3.   Jeremiah 23:29 *This is your signal/logo scripture for the entire book. Remember it.*

'Is not my word like fire', declares the Lord, *'and like a hammer that breaks a rock in pieces?'* You will use God's Word like a hammer to break in pieces that **wall of prayer-hindering rocks** called Self.

1... 2... 3... It's just that simple. The only really hard part is being honest with your Self when you are asked to identify your past and present heart attitudes. Then, you must be open to new ways of praying. Your old ways didn't work well. Right?

PRAY all the provided prayers *out loud* so that you can hear what you are saying. It will help you focus as you search your heart and allow the Holy Spirit to work within you.

READ all the scriptures *out loud* because faith comes when you hear the Word of God. God's spoken Word carries the power within it to strengthen your faith. Then your faith will grow as you *hear* yourself speak God's Word. For you see, only God's words, not your words have the power to transform. This God-kind of power is received by faith as you believe, but you must also confirm that belief by acting upon it.

Think about it! How many New Year's resolutions have you made in an attempt to change? How many firm resolutions have you succeeded in keeping? God's Word has the power within it to accomplish what God has spoken. If you want what God wants, and if you say what God says according to

His plan for your life, it is done — period! The catch is that you must know God's words and speak them in faith. Chew on that one for a while!

Matthew 21:21 *Jesus replied, "I tell you the truth, if you have faith and do not doubt...you can say to the mountain, 'Go throw yourself into the sea', and it will be done."*

Helpful hints for reading this book:
- Take your time.
- Meditate.
- Destroy one Self rock at a time.
- Pray
- Get your chosen scripture in your heart before you go on to the next challenge.

All scripture quoted here is in italics, the quotation marks have been omitted. All scriptures are from the New International Version (NIV) unless otherwise indicated. King James Version is noted as KJV. Amplified Version is noted as AMP.

Self is capitalized to indicate you, <u>personally</u>. It is not connected with a hyphen to a character trait or attitudes of the heart. For the purpose of focus on Self, the character trait is a separate word. Self is the part of you which holds back answer to prayer. When the trait and self are together with a hyphen they become a concept or idea. Small "s" spirit means *your* spirit. "S" Spirit is the Holy Spirit. He with a capital "H" refers to God and small "h" refers all others.

Remember. Your goal is to break the barrier rocks of Self which hold back answers to your prayers. When you break these barriers with the hammer of God's Word as in **Jeremiah 23:29**, you prepare the way to *Let God Answer Your Prayers*.

God bless you and give you insight into His truth as you read and pray.

Marion Clark

GOD ALWAYS ANSWERS

God answers prayer. He <u>really</u> does, even if you think that He doesn't. Your ignorance of how God works through prayer may be the major reason that you are not receiving your answers. There is more involved in answered prayer than just the act of praying. Your faith, your attitude, your relationship with God, and your knowledge of God's Holy Word, all have a critical effect on your prayers. If you pray only from your own need then you may be praying *impersonally*, expecting wise, loving answers from a stranger and not from your loving Father, Creator.

Most important to God is the condition of your heart. God sees your heart, which is the very essence of your being. His spirit judges its thoughts and attitudes. When you speak in prayer, you speak what is in your heart. God hears the words of your mouth which may originate in your intellect - not your heart. He hears what you're saying, but He *sees* your heart at the same time. If your heart is far from Him, and you haven't done your part according to His directions written in the Bible, you may *not* have received your answer. That doesn't mean that God didn't send the answer. You, your Self may have blocked reception by not recognizing it. God's answer may have been treated as junk mail which ends up in the trash because it wasn't what you were looking for. In effect, you refused God's answer. It didn't match *your* expectations. Examine how you pray. Have you ever been guilty of telling God what you wanted Him to do, or asking for something that He has already given you as clearly recorded in scripture? Why would He answer such prayers? Think about it.

COMMUNICATION WITH GOD BASICS 101

You were not born knowing how to talk intimately with God – you have to learn. *Everybody* has to learn. The disciples had been

5

praying in the Jewish tradition all of their lives, yet they asked Jesus to teach them to pray. Jesus taught them – in person. They learned God's way. You have been praying in some form all of your life, but you, like the disciples, may not have really learned God's way. Jesus sent the Holy Spirit to teach you – in person. You, too, will learn God's way through the guidance of the Holy Spirit and be just as effective in receiving answers as Jesus and the disciples were. Make answers to prayer your *heart's* desire. Don't be wimpy about it! Ask boldly! What He has promised to give you is ready, just awaiting your request. Read **Hebrews 4:16**

RECEIVING ANSWERS

God sends prayer answers *which often remain un-received*. He also does not receive prayers that are prayed out of Self-ish desires. Did you ever think that the problem lies not with the sender but the pray-er? God answered, maybe even years ago, but you are still waiting or you have given up. It's time to track your expected, undelivered messages to see why you didn't get them. Think of your prayers *and* their answers as letters lying in the dead letter office of the United States Postal Service. Did you fulfill the requirements for sending mail by supplying a readable address complete with zip code, proper amount of postage, and return address? In order to receive mail delivery, is your house number placed on the approved mail box? Did you move and not leave a forwarding address? *God has done His part. He is willing to hear your prayers and answer you.* If you didn't do your part, God may not have received your prayer or you may not have received His answer. There are right ways and wrong ways to do everything. Follow the rules – get results. Prayers get blocked on both ends, yours *and* God's. Ignorance of the rules and requirements may be the reason you are not communicating well with God.

DEAD LETTER PRAYERS

How many dead-letter prayers have you prayed? I know that I prayed the same prayer for ten years and never once recognized an answer. It was not until I figured out that I was praying the wrong prayer. (Duhhhhhh!) I thought all I had to do was ask and God would give me what I asked for. I was asking for the wrong things. So-- like a good father, He knows my needs, my weaknesses, my heart, and He won't give me something that will now or in the future cause me harm or harm the one for whom I am praying. Children in their ignorance, ask parents for things that would be bad for them. Kids may pitch a fit if they don't get exactly what they asked for, but they don't know enough to realize that they are being protected by being denied. Sometimes "silence" and "no" are answers. When I didn't get answers I thought something was wrong with God, that He was mad at me or punishing me, or at the very least, that He didn't know where I lived. For all those years, the dead-letter office was piling up my prayers that never reached God because I didn't know how to pray. I didn't know God personally, so how could I know His will for my life. I really didn't expect Him to answer me anyway.

When I finally got the message that it was *my* problem that prayers weren't answered and not God's, I figured that I just had to live without answers. Still, I kept praying those "lost in space prayers" to a distant God because I didn't know what else to do. Sunday school wasn't helping. Sermons on Sunday morning weren't helping. I just drifted. Then I got the idea to start searching for answers in the Bible. I tracked down two scriptures which brightened my pathway to answered prayer.

- **Matthew 6:33:** *But seek first his kingdom and his righteousness and all these things will be given to you as well.*

- **Psalm 37:4, 5:** *Delight yourself in the Lord and he will give you the desires of your heart. Commit your way to the Lord; trust in him and he will do this.* I liked the desires of your heart part.

I began doing what the Psalm and Matthew said by committing my ways, trusting, and seeking God first. I posted these scriptures on the refrigerator, on the dash in the car, and memorized them. When I began to seek a relationship with God, answers to my prayers began to come. Seeking God is really where answered prayer begins. I have never regretted my decision to seek God *first*. Before I made that decision to seek Him, nothing worked and I was totally miserable. I had no idea what peace, joy, and love could be mine, gladly given in abundance by my heavenly Father. My prayer life began in ignorance of God, and as I grew spiritually, I became increasingly dissatisfied with my old ways. I wanted to get closer to God now that I knew it was possible.

God has done His part. Have you done your part? If you don't know God's requirements, it's very possible that you haven't been receiving your answers. It's time to get serious. Track down what you are not doing according to God's will; start learning what God requires of you.

GOD'S REQUIREMENTS

Consider **Psalm 91:14, 15.** *Because he loves me, says the Lord, I will rescue him. I will protect him, for he acknowledges my name. He will call upon me, and I will answer him.*

Why should God answer prayers that don't fit His requirements? If you do not respect Him enough to learn what He wants and do as He requires, how can you grow in faith and love of God? Without fulfilling these three requirements in Psalm 91 (love, acknowledge, call) there can be no relationship with God which results in answered prayer. If God answered prayers not in His will, He would in effect be saying to you, "Live the way you want. In your ignorance, cause harm to yourself or others, and I will rubber stamp your lifestyle." The truth of the Bible would then be meaningless and absolutely useless.

YOUR PART is to 1) Love God, 2) Acknowledge God, 3) Call Upon Him. The dictionary says "call" means to cry aloud. You *can't* call in your thoughts. Use your voice.

GOD'S PART is to answer when you call. God doesn't lie. He promises in **Psalm 91** that His answers to you will be accomplished. Please finish reading Psalm 91. You will see that He promises:

8

- To answer you
- To protect you
- To rescue you
- To honor you
- To guard you
- To deliver you

- To give you salvation
- To command angels concerning you
- To be faithful to you
- To lift you up
- To save you from enemy traps
- To give you rest

Where else can you get such a bargain for the small price of three actions on your part? You get more than you ask for from God. But, still - what if you have not received God's promised answer? What happened? Did He not answer? Did He not hear? Was He not able to answer? None of the above.

Scripture tells you that God is well able to answer. He is not deaf, and He always answers. So, of course He answered. God does not lie. You did not receive the answer, because probably you did not *let* Him answer. Your own will, false beliefs, and ignorance of God's ways may be among the many possible reasons. In **Psalm 91** God's requirements must be met before you can receive the promised answers. This Psalm is not the only place where you will find God's requirements written. They occur over and over again many times in His Word. I never noticed them until I began seeking.

Summary of Requirements:

① Love God

② Acknowledge Him with faith and belief

③ Call to him with a willingness to submit to His will

Also in **Micah 6:8** scripture says: *He has showed you, O man, what is good. And what does the Lord require of you? To act justly and love mercy and to walk humbly with your God.*

Follow the directions in your guide book, the Bible in your hand. The directions work! God has proven His promises many times over in His faithfulness to protect and rescue me, personally. Because I believe and ask, I walk in safety and confidence, wherever I go. I do not fear falling, car accidents

9

and the like. When I have a "Whew, that-was-a-close-one" kind of experience which leaves me shaking, these words gratefully pop out of my mouth, "Thank you, God, for sending your angels to bear me up and protect me from harm." God will do the same for you -- if you believe and ask.

You have to realize that surviving a close call is not explained by coincidence, your horoscope, or that lucky rabbit's foot you carry. It is God doing what He has promised to do. You acknowledge Him by recognizing His faithfulness, *not* by explaining away any supernatural intervention of God as coincidence, the natural order of things, or luck. Are you aware that God watches over you - always? Does your belief system need a "faith tune-up"?

My faith desperately needed a tune-up. I wasn't always aware of God's presence in my life. I thought of Him as being distant, rather than right beside me. I didn't know Him spiritually, I just knew *about* Him intellectually. Reading the Psalms helps me to get closer to Him to the place where I will sometimes just stop and marvel at His faithfulness. I often look up to heaven and say, "God, just how many times *have* You saved me?" Then I answer myself, "I can't count that high!" Mostly, I don't even realize until some time afterwards that it was God who stepped in and protected me.

I am blessed by God's love. It takes being aware of His presence daily, acknowledging Him and calling upon Him to receive all that God has promised *in addition* to answering your prayers. God is generously giving you overflowing answers, not just enough, but more than enough. He is willing to give you everything. Remember He gave His son, Jesus, to die for you.

He created everything out of love, out of Himself, for God is love. Why then should He be stingy? He made everything. To understand the full measure of God's love, Read **1 Corinthians Chapter 13**, the Love Chapter. There is no evil intent or selfishness in love. *All* love comes from God.

REVIEW!! YOUR PART as stated in **Psalm 91:**
1) Love God. 2) Acknowledge God. 3) Call out to Him.

I repeat the requirements so that you won't forget. Live with **Psalm 91** in your heart and on your lips. Doing so will increase your spiritual strength and your faith. The more faith you have, the more you please God. His Word says, *without faith it is impossible to please Him.* If your desire is to please Him, then His desire is to fulfill His promises of: answers, *plus:* protection, rescue, deliverance, salvation, faithfulness, honor, guardian angels, warnings of traps, and rest.

If, perhaps, you think God's unpredictability is the reason your prayers seem to go unanswered, you do not know Him. How can you love and trust someone whom you do not know? God never changes. What He says He will do, He does. God didn't drop the ball and fail to answer you. The one holding back the answers to your prayers is you. It may be out of ignorance of God's requirements. It may be a difference between your understanding of time and God's understanding. But, it's *your* responsibility to read the directions that come with the Bible, which is your How-to-Receive-from-God, instruction book.

BELIEF MAKE-OVER

If you want to find out what you're doing wrong or what false beliefs you are applying in your life, match your belief with scripture. Some things which people believe are in the Bible are not there. They are false. You can never know what God requires if you don't match your beliefs with His Word. A common example of a false belief is: "God helps those who help themselves". This is *not* in the Bible.

GAINING UNDERSTANDING WHEN READING GOD'S WORD

If you don't understand the version of the Bible that you are presently using, go to a Christian bookstore where you will find many translations. Choose the one that makes sense to you. Even when you have a more understandable translation, it may take more than one reading to understand how it applies to your life. Many versions have helpful notes for those times. A determined mindset will help you succeed. After all, God *does* want you to understand His Word. Right? Pray to Him asking for that understanding, then stay with it, expecting to succeed. You will.

It's worth your time to work on understanding God's directions first. Did you get it? If not, re-read the passage again. Did you mis-read? Did you skip something? Did you have a part missing or add an extra part? Did you misinterpret, relying on what you think you know or think you have read? Did you believe what someone told you that took God's words out of context? Is it possible that you read one thing, but thought something else. If so, read out loud and listen to yourself. Hearing what you say is often helpful.

Most people don't object to double-checking directions when something is not going together or working right. By going back and re-reading directions again, you finally get the right information for tasks such as: recipes, appliance installations and the trouble shooting guide on the computer. Why not use this same tenacity to get answers to understanding scriptures and praying? God tells us to seek and we will find His will.

MEDITATE FOR MEANING

Do you know how to meditate on God's Word? God clearly tells you to meditate on His Word day and night in **Psalm 1**. Read it. Meditation works something like a stone polisher cylinder for a gems and minerals hobbyist. You place the uncut, unfinished semi-precious rock [scripture sentence, phrase, or idea] into a rotating polishing cylinder [in the back of your mind] and let it tumble for a while [as you sleep or do some mindless chore]. Check on it occasionally as it polishes. Your spirit will do the work of the gem polisher as it uncovers understanding which results in a shining smooth gem stone [your understanding]. Then thank God for helping you. Patience and persistence work together with the Spirit in God's word to give you understanding.

Now you're really succeeding and growing! Re-read, check yourself and meditate. Why would God withhold wisdom and understanding when He asks you to seek it? Hummm? Go back and re-read the directions. Receive your prayer answers by:

1. Removing any obstructions such as your Self, which you placed between you and God.
2. Believing that God will perform His Word as promised.
3. Acknowledging God's will as you meditate on and gain understanding of His Word.

Now that you know how to do your part, expect to get results. Receive His answers - not a rubber stamp of yours.

It's just that 1...2...3...simple.

NOW CHECK YOURSELF FOR UNBELIEF

When you don't expect to receive answers, of course that attitude is reflected in your choice of words used in prayer. Watch carefully to be sure that you are not praying in unbelief with words such as: "IF it is your will"... Forget your answer to *that* prayer. You need to know His will so that you will not doubt. When you pray without knowing God's will, you may be asking something that God cannot do because He has said in His word that He *would not* do it. Don't waste your time in prayers which are ignorant of God's will.

If you are not praying, asking according to God's will, nothing is going to happen. If you don't know what His will is, you're just guessing. How then can you have faith to receive an answer? Think what chaos would be loosed if God answered, "Yes" to all your prayers. It would be as if someone like you who doesn't know the first thing about the order and accuracy of running a universe, is guessing at orbits of planets, length of seasons, how long it takes seeds to sprout, and how many baby rabbits fit into the finely balanced food chain.

You gotta' go with God's plans because, if left to your wisdom, everything on the planet and in your life would be chaos. Is it in chaos now? Do you have God's peace? Are things more right with your life than wrong? Or is it the other way around?

BELIEF IN GOD'S AWESOME WISDOM

If you think that you don't deserve to be answered because you are so sinful or unworthy, then you are not believing that Jesus paid the price for your sins. Which, by the way, makes you a non-Christian or an unbeliever.

How can you ask for anything in Jesus' name? You have to believe God's word and *trust* in His wisdom, then you can anticipate delivery of over-flowing answers. You will not - no - cannot receive answers from God if you try to bargain or manipulate God to get what you want. Get the division of labor straight! You are the servant. He is your loving Master and Creator. Submit to His will and all things fall into place. In other words, Butt out! I know. That's about as hard as keeping your fingers out of the chocolate icing! But - it's your choice.

Here's the bottom line: in **Matthew 6:33.** God promises that if you ...*Seek first the kingdom of God, and his righteousness; and all these things shall be added unto you.* Seek God first –not Self. His way – not your way. Then *all* things are added.

SELF-DECEPTION

Before you begin to closely examine how you, yourself are holding back your prayer answers, take a look at an old enemy — self-deception.

Be aware! Your ego will not like the change of focus from Self to God. Self is used to running things and making all the decisions. It will try to tell you that you are fine just the way you are, that you are being honest with yourself, and that there is no deception in you. It will tell you that you don't have time to read your scripture which tells you that if you say that you are not deceived then you are deceived already. Trust God's Word <u>only</u> for eternal truth. Pray first that the Holy Spirit will guide you into truth about your Self. Without that revelation of truth, you will not be able to identify and address any Self issues which are the roots of unanswered prayer.

Remember your responsibility for achieving the goal of answered prayer.
1. Love God.
2. Believe and have faith to receive from Him.
3. Submit your will to God's will and receive the help of the Holy Spirit.

That is the tough part. Submitting to God's will takes desire and determination to overcome your dependency upon Self for your well-being.

REMOVE SELF FROM BLOCKING UNDERSTANDING
Read out loud the following scriptures. After each one pray, and declare out loud that you believe what you have just heard yourself say.

- In **John 3:30** (AMP), John the Baptist said: *He [Jesus] must increase, but I must decrease. He must grow more prominent, and*

I must grow less prominent.

PRAY: *I want more of you, Jesus, and less of me (my Self). Amen*

- In **1 Corinthians 3:18, 19**, God's Word says: *Do not deceive yourselves. If anyone of you thinks he is wise by the standards of this age, he should become a "fool" so that he may become wise. For the wisdom of the world is foolishness in God's sight. . .*

  PRAY: *I repent of deceiving my Self by acting in my own wisdom at times when I spoke or acted without the wisdom of God. Amen.*

- In **Jeremiah 17:9** (AMP) God says: *The heart is deceitful above all things and is exceedingly perverse and corrupt and severely mortally sick. Who can know it* (that is ...*be acquainted with, perceive, understand with his own heart and mind)?* Also read **Matthew 13:15-17:** *The people's heart has become calloused.*

  PRAY: *Help me to know when my heart is deceitful, Lord: Make my heart tender to Your loving touch. Teach me to discern between Your clear voice and my Self deceptions. Pour out Your Holy Spirit on me, for I am not able to succeed without His help. Amen*

Do not let intellect or false belief motivate you to take **offense** at God's Truth. Determine in your spirit to remove whatever self-centered attitudes block reception of prayer answers. Your relationship to God will become stronger, and your Self influence will diminish in its ability to control your thought patterns.

WORLDLY TEACHINGS EMPOWER THE **SELF**

When you subscribe to the world's trust *in*, and value *of*, personal strength, you live as if you, your Self are its source. You scorn dependency of any kind as weakness and fall into spiritual Self-deception. For you have chosen <u>not</u> to look foolish in the eyes of the world by relying upon God in times of trouble. Unbelievers as well as Christians would surely ask you, "Where is God now?", "Why did God let this happen?", and most often of all, "Why doesn't God answer?" To live your life depending upon God in a world that does not know Him, appears to be foolish, weak, and powerless. No one wants to be laughed at. You do not want to be judged as foolish for trusting in God, because you greatly value what people think of you. There is deception in the belief that you, a Christian, can "fit in" to a society that lives without loving, acknowledging and praying to God. You have to live what you believe, or be as the Pharisees Jesus called "white sepulchers" They were knowing, yet not believing. Read **Matthew 23:27.**

Here is a classic poem once taught in public schools. This last stanza of "Invictus", written by William Ernest Henley, will give you an understanding of why you as an American are so strongly centered upon Self.

> "It matters not how strait the gate,
>   How charged with punishments the scroll,
>   I am the master of my fate;
>   I am the captain of my soul."

You are unaware that things taught to you in your youth are still reflected in our Self choices and attitudes today. I marvel that I could remember "Invictus" some 50 years later. Now, when I am older and wiser in God's Word, I can recognize the Self-deception in this poem.

Ideas instilled at an early age by people who are in authority over you die hard. They often oppose the submission to the will of God in glorifying the strength and power of Self-determination. I bought it. I believed the poem's message and the teacher who taught it. I thought that it was a great poem because I liked the idea of being "in charge". It pumped up my youthful pride. I regret that God's Word was not taught to me with as much love and dedication as was high school literature. During my teaching career, I advanced this same secular knowledge with just as much enthusiasm. At that time, my spiritual life was strictly separate from my secular life. I was deceived and didn't know it. Deception is exposed by the truth of God's Word which, regrettably, I read only on Sunday. That's why it is so important to read or hear scripture early in life, so that you have the Truth of God's Word to match with and expose worldly deceptions. It's much harder to do it the other way around when your worldly belief system is firmly entrenched. Better to learn God's Word before you learn the ways of the world so that God's truth is your basis for comparison. Now we have the Holy Spirit to guide us into all Truth. Rely upon Him.

PRAY: *Lord, open my spiritual eyes to identify any deception that I have previously accepted as truth for my life. I desire to know You and Your Truth.* AMEN (firm and established.)

A WORD ABOUT AMEN

You probably wondered why I added firm and established after the Amen. Since you will be praying a lot, you have need of a new understanding of the meaning of the word "Amen". No, it does not mean, "We're done now." or "So be it."

"Amen" means firm and established. According to the <u>New Westminster Dictionary of the Bible</u>. Martin Luther said that "Amen" should mean:

"That I should be assured that such petitions are acceptable to our Heavenly Father and are heard by Him, for He himself has commanded us to pray in this manner and has promised that He will hear us."

So don't just tack "Amen" on at the end of your prayer. **Know** that you believe and are firmly establishing these things that you have just prayed.

EXPLORING THE MEANING OF SELF

While searching for a specific word meaning for a phrase in my writing, I often use the <u>Webster's Dictionary and Thesaurus for Home, School, and Office</u>. This helps me to nail down exactly what I intend to say. It was during this process that I discovered an entry which took up more space than probably any other in the entire dictionary. Almost one fourth of a page was dedicated to over thirty-one hyphenated "self" words. Immediately, it hit me that these words are the spiritual disconnect answer I had been looking for regarding why people depend upon themselves and not God. There it was-- "Self" right in front of me 31 times. I selected twenty-three of these words for further exploration and, of course, God being His wonderfully generous self, taught me far more than enough to fill the short twenty-five pages I had first intended to write.

The following is a sample list of Self words: Self-determination, Self-reliant, Self-indulgent, Self-willed, Self-sufficient, Self-help, Self-respect, Self defense. I capitalize Self and separate it without the hyphen because Self actually identifies you specifically as a person. With the hyphen, it becomes a concept.

SELF WAS NOT THE BASIS FOR OUR AMERICAN INDEPENDENCE

In American culture many Self words are considered positive and advantageous -- even desirable character traits. I grew up with self-image, self-confidence, and self-defense and I, in turn taught these things to my children. Since then , God's Word has taught me how deceptive worldly standards of independence can be when they exclude God and rise above and beyond the need of wartime patriotism. You were taught to focus so much upon your own individual liberties that there is danger in becoming so self-focused that you are blind to the source of true liberty. Americans are a people proud of their independence and   ability to pull themselves up by their own bootstraps. But, by focusing on your own individuality, not the unity of national strength, Self-reliance can become an unrecognized imprisonment, a spiritual yoke, an idol, restraining you from reaching your true spiritual freedom in Jesus. You are a part of the church, which is the body of Christ in unity with God. To focus on, and strictly function in your own individuality, is to deny your spiritual heritage and create a disunity in government by seeing only one need and point of view — your own.

The strength that Americans rely upon today, taught by and embedded in the culture, is independence **apart** from God. We rely on strength of Self, not God's strength. Remember that the foundations of religious freedom came from people submitted and committed to serving God. To what do Americans submit today? The individual was important at our foundation because of Jesus' sacrifice on the cross to redeem each one of us back to a relationship with God. God is not willing for even one to be lost. The importance of the individual is ingrained in Americans.

Today, individual rights reign supreme over all. We have deviated from our original purpose and forgotten unity under God. Unity is a problem for us as Americans because we are each going our separate ways to fulfill our own dreams independent of God and others. Yes! America is governmentally free and independent from tyranny. NO! America must **not be** spiritually independent from God.

SERVING SELF OR SERVING GOD
A CHOICE

Self, in a spiritual context, is sometimes called "flesh" which brings you into unavoidable conflict with God's perfect principles and standards as written in His inspired Word. I didn't see anything wrong with "self" words, because I never looked at them from a spiritual angle. I didn't know that most of them, at least the twenty-three I selected, are contrary to what God's Word teaches. I didn't know the truth of God's Word for purposes of comparison.

These Self words are at the same time attractive and deceptive to the point of creating a dual nature within you. Do you depend upon God, or do you depend upon your Self? Do you try to do things your Self and - then failing in that - give God a try at it? Do you depend entirely upon God as risky as it may sound, or do you keep doing things your own familiar but ineffective way? How can you live a victorious, prayerful life if you are focused on your cultural self-focused nature every day of the week except Sunday?

SELF PRAYERS

Self-focus has de-railed your prayers. If you want answers to your prayers, you have to stop relying on Self and rely only upon God. Is it possible that you have had such frustrated thoughts as: "I'm tired of waiting for God. He's not answering so I'm going to do something!" What's wrong here? In the first place, you prayed in doubt. In the second place, you became afraid and lost trust in God. In the third place, you don't want to wait; you are desperate for answers now.

Everything in this world today seems to focus on Self. You're so accustomed to using your own wisdom for making choices and as the sole source of answers to problems, that you forget the reason why you believe that God sent Jesus to save you in the first place. You live a double life - one mostly for Self, and what's left over, is lived for God. You cannot serve two masters. The Bible tells you that you have to make a choice. Now is the time to choose. If you want answers to your prayers, you have to _stop relying on your Self_ and rely only on God. Scary? Yes! Worth the effort? Absolutely!

DOUBLE-MINDED ISRAELITES

You can't have it both ways-- yours and God's. The chosen people of God, the Israelites, had the problem of double mindedness. Learn from their example in the Old Testament:

In the wilderness, the Israelites tried to serve both God and the comfort of "flesh" in the form of their old gods. It didn't work. In their fear and impatience, they prevailed upon their spiritual leader, Aaron, to create a golden calf out of the Egyptian gold that God had provided for them. Then, when they didn't see Moses coming down from the holy mountain of God, they worshipped this golden man-made image. Is it possible that you, like the Israelites, have been attempting to provide answers for your own prayers, being too fearful and impatient to wait for God? The Israelites are a prime example of always having a "Plan B". They were constantly moving into and out of God's favor because they could not "Wait on the Lord". They could not serve two masters. They tried! Read the whole story in **Exodus 32.**

Are you any different? Do you wait on the Lord, trusting that no matter how long it takes that He will do what He has promised, or do you attempt to answer your own prayers by returning to your former ways of depending upon Self motivated by fear and unbelief? Fifteen times in similar form, God's Word says, "Be strong and of good courage." If you didn't have trials that required strength and courage, then why would God keep encouraging you to have it? You *will* have trials that test your strength and courage. You can go through them *with* God's help or *without* God's help. Your choice.

Deuteronomy 31:6 says, *Be strong and courageous. Do not be afraid or terrified because of them for the Lord your God goes with you; He will never leave you nor forsake you.* God also says to wait *on* Him and *for* Him.

Micah 7:7 *But as for me I watch in hope for the Lord, I wait for God my Savior; my God will hear me.* David the psalmist says over and over, "Wait upon the Lord". David pleased God greatly. He waited on the Lord. Impatience will get you into trouble because it is acting in unbelief and Self will. If you do not believe that God will do what He says He will do, you have chosen to trust in your own judgment – your Self.

Notice how often you cross the line back and forth between Self and God. Frustrated thoughts, even thoughts of desperation such as: "I'm tired of waiting for God". "Things are falling apart here". "I can't hang on and wait for God much longer". "If I don't get an answer by Monday, I'm going to do something my Self". "God will have to do something soon!" What's going on here? Something inside you tells you that you're on the wrong track, but you don't know how to get on the right track.

GETTING TO KNOW GOD IS
THE RIGHT TRACK

It's easy to <u>ascribe your own personal failings and feelings to God</u>. You may suggest to your Self that He, God would act in a human-like manner instead of the Creator of all things. Thoughts like the following may appear like the TV crawlers unconsciously inching their way across the bottom of the screen of your consciousness. "God forgot. He's angry with me. He's punishing me. He's teaching me a lesson. He doesn't understand. I'm not good enough. He's asking too much of me. He's given up on me". Every one of these statements *does not apply to God* under the New Covenant established by the sacrifice of Jesus on the cross.

You have to get to know God, how He works, what He wants, what pleases Him, but most of all you have to learn that <u>He is not a gigantic projection of your Self</u>. You are the clay and God is the Potter. How can you presume to tell the Potter how to mold you or question His perfect will for you?

PRAYER--A TWO-WAY RELATIONHIP

Do you need and want a relationship with God? Do you know how to build this desired bond with God? *Prayer is a two- way relationship originally initiated by God, but daily practiced by you.* He waits for you to call upon Him in prayer. He does not check on you periodically like a good waiter in a restaurant. Without your asking, a waiter appears, whisks away your empty plate and refills your drink glasses. He asks, "How is everything? Can I get you something else? The waiter's desire is to please you and see that your needs are met. That is *not* God's job to come to you. God is not the servant. However, it is His choice and His joy to supply for all of your needs. The difference is that <u>He</u> waits for <u>you</u> to seek <u>Him</u>. He invites you to come partake of His glorious blessings, but it has to be *your desire* to come to Him-- **first**.

Explore who God is, and you'll have more to talk about than your Self next time you pray. Prayer is an interaction and understanding between you and God. There is love and trust for one another flowing back and forth. If you're not there yet - in prayer partnership with God - then work on it! Get to know your Creator. He may just tell you a few wonderful things about your Self that you haven't yet discovered. In other words, seek God for Who He is because you want to know Him and not what He can do for you. Both partners receive and enjoy. God desires to talk with you. He wants you to come to Him in prayer. His Word in **James 4:8** says, *Draw near to God and He will draw near to you.* You draw near to God through Jesus, when you pray in Jesus' name.

Gene MacLellan wrote a popular song in the 70's titled "Put Your Hand in the Hand". It's all about trusting Jesus to lead you to God, your Father. When you put your hand in Jesus' hand, you put your Self behind you and trust Jesus to lead you. Jesus intercedes to the Father for you day and night. Trust Him - not your Self.

> Put your hand in the hand of the man who stilled the water.
> Put your hand in the hand of the man who calmed the sea.
> Take a look at yourself and you can look at others differently
> By puttin' your hand in the hand of the man from Galilee.

GETTING TO KNOW YOUR "SELF"

Examine your motives, attitudes, and expectations and discover how your Self has placed prayer hindrances between you and God.

1. Motives for Prayer Think about why you pray. How is your relationship to God reflected in your motives? Ask your Self if this is the kind of relationship you want to have with God. Why do you pray?

Because you need something
> OR because you love God?

Gene MacLellan song, "Put Your Hand in the Hand", 1970

Because you are afraid
>OR do you trust God and have faith in Him?

Because you feel helpless in a situation
>OR do you feel empowered by God?

Because you are suffering in pain and grief
>OR do you feel God's love for you?

Because you need help
>OR do you want to give Him thanks and praise?

Because you need to do your daily prayer
>OR do you miss talking to God?

Remember that prayer is a relationship and by definition, it takes more than one participant.

You talk -
>He listens

He talks -
>You listen

Speak words of love to Him -
>He speaks words of love to you

You express your troubles and fears -
>He comforts and shares His heart with you

You express your joys and sing to Him -
>He responds with love to you

You delight yourself (take pleasure) in Him -
>He takes pleasure in you

It's a giving and receiving thing for both you and God. Prayer is a loving relationship/conversation with your Heavenly Father.

2. Attitudes of Prayer

Do you pray in faith believing that you receive what you have

prayed for *OR*
    do you pray in unbelief not expecting answers?

Do you pray to a loving Father expecting to receive the good gifts that His Word promises *OR*
    do you bargain and manipulate to get God to give you what you want?

Do you pray God's will in humbleness *OR*
    do you pray in pride recounting all the things you have done for God, expecting rewards for your deeds?

Do you pray desperately, passionately for God to move and make changes in your life and the lives of others *OR*
    do you want Him to rubber stamp your worldly comfort and pleasure prayers or prayer requests that you make for others?

Do you pray in an attitude of Love *OR*
    do you pray in fear and doubt?

3. <u>Expectations of Prayer</u> - These questions are designed to help you think about your prayer life from many angles and to see other possibilities that you have not yet tried.

- Do you hope, or are you sure that God's answers will come?
- Do you keep track of your prayers in some form of journaling so that you expect and know when you receive specific answers?
- Do you sometimes get answers, but you're not sure whether it is God answering or it is your imagination?
- Do you wonder why others seem to get answers, but you don't hear from God?
- Do you expect to wait a long time, maybe years, for answers, or do you expect to hear clearly and quickly?
- Do you fear expecting answers because of possible disappointment?
- When you pray, do you expect to feel something happen, and if you don't feel anything, then you think that God did not hear or answer your prayer?

- When you don't get answers, do you give up, or do you keep on praying until you get answers?

Not everything works the same for every pray-er. Each person has a special prayer relationship with God. Have you tried to be like someone else whom you consider to be more "spiritual" than you are? Stop it!! Follow Jesus and not another *man* who may or may not be "spiritual". Be yourself with God. You cannot copy someone else's prayer style. Paul tells us not to compare ourselves spiritually with anyone. Have you felt defeated because your prayers didn't go anywhere? Think about where and how you can improve your prayer relationship with God. Learn what He requires so that you can agree with Him. When you agree with God's will according to His purposes for your life, you know that He will answer prayer. **Being in agreement with God in prayer is powerful.**

God is an orderly God. Seed time and harvest and all of nature run in their proper order. Even as nature has rules, so does God have rules for prayer spelled out just as clearly in His Word. There are many examples of prayers in the Bible to teach you how to pray effectively. You can experience powerful prayer once you understand and follow God's requirements. Explore the prayers of the Bible in the Old Testament in the Psalms and those in the New Testament especially prayers prayed by Jesus and Paul.

PRAYER OF PREPARATION

It is important to pray before you begin examining your Self. It will try to hinder your prayers. Things get uncomfortable when you start digging around in unfamiliar territory. You have a built-in alarm system, which protects your "sore spots" without thinking, much like you would favor a sprained ankle. Formerly accepted deceptions can be revealed by this alarm.

Are you really determined to uncover those deceptions of Self which block your prayers? Are you ready to let God answer you prayers? If so, you have to <u>turn off your alarm system and</u>

"get real". Get painfully honest! SELF DECEPTION will try to block your way and may cause you to take offense at God's Word or react in anger and unbelief. There are 149 references to deception including all its forms and spellings in Strong's Exhaustive Concordance of the Bible. God is really serious about the "deception" thing and Self-deception reigns supreme at the top of the list. Deal with it first. Know that you can be deceived into believing that you are not deceived. Pray from your heart not from your mind. Pray out loud and be open to what the Holy Spirit may reveal to you during your prayer. Add to the following prayer your own personal requests and vulnerabilities regarding deception.

PRAY the following out loud:
> Loving God, I know that You will lead me into all truth by the Holy Spirit, for that is the work Jesus sent Him to do in me. Whenever I try to deceive my Self, warn me by showing me the Truth of Your Word. Keep me spiritually alert so that my heart may not deceive me. It is a tough task which I have chosen to begin, but the prayer-power I gain in You is well worth my effort. I need Your help, strength, wisdom, and guidance. I ask You for clear spiritual sight and wisdom unclouded by Self-deception. In Jesus' mighty name I pray. AMEN (firm and established.)

Look through this list of Self words again.   Can you see them from a spiritual, scriptural, point of view now?

Self-determination	Self-sufficient
Self-reliant	Self-help
Self-indulgent	Self-respect
Self-willed	Self-defense

Have you begun to see how each Self word stands as a part of an impenetrable rock wall between you and God? Match the concepts of defense, will, sufficiency etc. with scripture that you know. Where is commitment to God in these words? How many of these words have you used to describe your Self or to achieve your goals and desires? You may have built a strong rock wall of pride and Self-focus between you and God.

DIG UNTIL YOU GET TO THE TRUTH
THEN---- PRAY IT

When you subscribe to the worldly concepts of doing everything for your Self and glory in the fact that you were able to do it, you are excluding God as your source of strength, peace, or comfort. The world teaches that depending upon a source other than your Self is immaturity, free-loading, weakness, laziness, even co-dependency. The world's way is opposite to God's way. It is spiritual deception to think that you can live both ways. If you pray worldly-focused, motivated prayers for foolish or selfish purposes, God cannot answer these prayers. He would be helping you to destroy your Self. Because God loves you, He cannot do that! Often an answer to a seemingly unanswered prayer is, "*NO*" or "Try again, praying according to My Word..." or "I'm listening". "Pray again after you have a change of heart and pray in Love..." or "Work on your prayer motivation until you get it right" or "Don't go away mad and don't give up. Read My Word and find out what you're praying wrong then change your prayer". God's silence may mean that you've got something spiritually wrong. **Find out what it is and fix it**. God is patient, but He doesn't change the rules to accommodate you. Remember you are the clay. He is the Potter. You cannot tell God how to make the pot. What does clay know? You have no vision of the final pot.

When you are not depending upon God for anything, but rather on your own strength and wisdom for everything, you have entered into the proud belief of the poet, Henley: "I am the master of my fate, the captain of my soul". How can you be a Christian *in* the world but not *of* the world unless you love and trust God and unless you have broken the deceptive barrier of Self?

WISDOM AND FOOLISHNESS

Paul says in **1 Corinthians 1:25**, *For the foolishness of God is wiser than man's wisdom, and the weakness of God is stronger than man's strength*. Remember, you as a believer are not subject to the opinions (judgments) of unbelievers. They don't know what they're talking about. Anyone who does not have the Spirit of

God is not qualified to judge the spiritual person. God's Word is the only standard of truth by which you can be judged. So in effect, God is your *only* judge.

Living your faith is not easy. The media mocks and accuses Christians. I was amazed at how an evangelist being interviewed on a national television news special was reminded that he had been a drug addict. He was asked to justify his shady past. I admired his faith in God as he stood before the cameras on a nationwide broadcast, and to the amazement of the interviewer, he did not rise to defend himself in any way. He admitted that what was said about him *was* true.

What the interviewer could not comprehend was how this man's ministry could cause such an uproar in Florida with healings, miracles, and people standing in line for hours just to get into the church where this former drug addict was speaking. The interviewer was "clueless" because worldly standards do not fit spiritual facts.

1 Corinthians 3:19 *For the wisdom of this world is foolishness in God's sight.*

1 Corinthians 2:14 *The man without the Spirit does not accept the things that come from the Spirit of God for they are foolishness to him, and he cannot understand them, because they are spiritually discerned.* This scripture is the clearest example I have ever seen representing how the world perceives and even mocks God.

Godly things make no sense to the unbeliever. Your words will not convince him to believe. It has to be by the work of the Holy Spirit. They, regardless of their intelligence, cannot explain what they cannot comprehend. You serve God, not man. You serve in power, not weakness. You have spiritual power and strength, but the world which focuses on strength of Self sees only weakness and foolishness in you. Self-comfort, self- advancement, self-honor are the goals of the world. Yes, the world may honor people like Mother Theresa, but no <u>worldly</u> person wants to be like her or live that life of compassion and sacrifice.

WHAT YOU CAN LEARN FROM JOB

The best example of how to thrive spiritually in a faithless world is in the book of Job. He was a man of faith favored by having such an intimate friendship with God that his whole house was blessed to the 4th generation. He lacked *nothing*. When the hard times came, he lost everything; his family, property, health, and wealth. He prayed a lot and continued to believe God.

The "patience of Job" that you may have heard about is not true. Job was <u>im</u>patient, and sometimes angry with God. The point of the book of Job is-- the Faith of Job in God's faithfulness manifested within a faith-<u>less</u>, self-centered world. He was pressured on all sides to curse God, but Job's faith did not weaken. He stood fast continuing to talk with God. He even prayed for those friends who verbally abused him.

Few of us will have to face such trials, but the lesson is clear: the world will pressure you to give up on God during trials, but if you remain faithful, He will accept your prayers. Read **Job 42:9.** The Lord made Job prosperous again, and at the end of the book, everything was restored over and above what Job had before. He and all of his family were greatly blessed. <u>He never lost touch with God.</u> Do not let Self or others tempt you to move away from God. Hang in there! Don't give up too soon! God is faithful. Keep the prayer lines open whether you feel like it or not

Job 42:12,16 says *The Lord blessed the latter part of Job's life more than the first. After this, Job lived 140 years...and so he died old and full of years.* The powerlessness as seen by the world, was in reality a great strength of faith which it did not understand. God rewards faith in many examples throughout the Bible. *And without faith it is impossible to please God, because anyone who comes to him must believe that He exists and that He rewards those who earnestly seek Him,* as in **Hebrews 11:6.**

You, as a Christian, stand God-reliant, God-defended, God-willed, God-conscious - if you let Him strengthen you. Above all else you must be God-confident and God-empowered. Of course, you have to do your part. God will not override your freedom to choose to be Self-confident and Self-empowered. God can only empower you if you allow Him to work through you and in you according to His Word. Put your Self-seeking behind you and faithfully seek God. Job's prayers were answered to the "full".

REVISIT PSALM 91

Re-read all of **Psalm 91** out loud again and sort it into two parts, YOUR PART and GOD'S PART. The Bible is full of agreements with God, but I never noticed them until recently. For everything that God promises as His part, there is a corresponding responsibility for you to perform in order to receive His glorious promises.

As before, your part is to Love God (believe and have faith) acknowledge Him, call to Him, and be willing and obedient (submit to His will). He responds by answering prayers and providing for all your needs.

SEEKING A NEW ATTITUDE OF PRAYER

Rely on God's Word as your guide for your prayers. Look at how you're praying now. Leave the old way behind, and try a new way of seeking the Lord, perhaps pray something that was generated from your reading so far.

Strive for the development of a new attitude of trust and single-mindedness. Get out of your former prayer pattern and look to succeed in receiving answers to prayer in a new way. Form a new attitude of expectancy for strength, fervency, and power in your prayers. Get excited about praying. Prayer is a joy. Being in God's presence is not a chore. God makes your heart sing and your legs to leap among the high places of the mountains. Realize that Jesus sent the Holy Spirit to teach you and guide you. He'll even pray through you when you don't know how to pray. Talk to the Holy Spirit. Ask Him to teach you some new thing about prayer. Invite the Holy Spirit to lead and empower your prayers. There is no limit to the power of prayer. Just getting answers is only the beginning. There's much, much more. How much do you want? Pray with a new attitude, a new strength of faith and expectancy now that you know there is **more**.

Seek to understand and recall **James 1:6-8.**

But when he asks he must believe and not doubt, because he who doubts is like a wave of the sea, blown and tossed by the wind. That man should not think he will receive anything from the Lord; he is a double-minded man unstable in all he does.

Here are some further suggestions to help you shift into a new attitude:

- Do not be satisfied with your present prayer attitude and pattern. GROW!
- Be single-minded, praying confidently in faith, believing.
- Read **Matthew 17:20** and then memorize **Matthew 21:21 and 22** from the Parable of the Fig Tree.
- Get a prayer partner and agree in prayer together. There is extra strength in the unity of agreement with another believer.
- Boldly call down God's will into your expectations

Jesus said … *I tell you the truth, if you have faith as small as a mustard seed, you can say to the mountain 'Move from here to there and it will move.' Nothing will be impossible for you.* **Matthew 17:20.**

Now that's exciting faith! With promises like these, why should you be struggling just to get answers to prayer? You're missing something. Ask God to give you the faith as small as a mustard seed. Then believe that He will give it to you. Earnestly desire that faith. Believe that when you ask for faith since it is definitely according to God's will, He will give it to you. God wants you to have faith in the power of prayer, <u>but you have to want it and ask for it.</u>

Before you continue - PRAY. Confess and ask forgiveness for

the doubts and unbelief you have expressed in past prayers. Determine to no longer be double-minded, but rather be single, God–minded. Trust God for His perfect answers-- PERIOD! <u>No plan B</u> if you think that you're not getting what you're asking for. Search your heart to see if you are praying according to God's will. Make changes and then pray again differently until you have a sense of peace and completeness rise up in you. Trust the Holy Spirit to teach you and even bring words or scriptures to your mind as you persevere in prayer. *Remember: pray out loud!*

PRAY: *Almighty God, I confess that I have often used You for insurance just in case I didn't get what I wanted any other way. I have done every thing my Self and consulted You as an afterthought. I have relied upon my Self for decisions without concern as to whether or not they are in agreement with Your Holy Word or Your will for me.. Lord, I ask to be able to hear Your Holy Spirit in me telling me where there is TRUTH AND WHERE THERE IS A SELF-DECEPTION. As I explore the depths of my soul, I intend to search for the rocks of Self that separate me from You and Your will. AMEN* (firm and established)

JEREMIAH 23:29
IS THE KEY SCRIPTURE OF
THIS ENTIRE BOOK

USE GOD'S WORD TO MAKE CHANGES

"Is not my Word like a fire," declares the Lord,
"and like a hammer that breaks a rock in pieces?"

This scripture is your hammer, your weapon, to break the prayer-hindering rocks of Self that you have placed between you and God. Then scripture tells you...*be transformed by the renewing of your minds.* Read **Romans 12:2.** *Do not conform any longer to the pattern of this world, but be transformed by the renewing of your mind. Then you will be able to test and approve what God's will is---His good, pleasing and perfect will.* Remember that you have the help of the **resurrection power of the Holy Spirit** to make changes. With each change from Self–empowered to God-empowered, you increase in prayer-power, authority, wisdom, love, joy, and peace, and above all, your relationship with your Creator.

THE POWER OF PERSISTANT HAMMERING

I read a report about a hammer and a cement wall that amazed me. If you take a sledge hammer and swing it at a weakened place in a cement wall, hit it continually over and over in the same place until a crack appears, then keep hitting it where you see the cracks spread, you will eventually succeed in breaking any strong, thick wall into a pile of rubble. Impossible? Remember the battering rams and catapults used by the Greeks and Romans in the historic sieges of walled cities? The persistent, forceful pounding of the siege machines created a wide gap in strong, thick walls. The hammer of God's Word works like a siege machine. It can destroy the hindering rocks of Self that hold back your prayer answers.

NEW STRATEGY FOR BOOSTING YOUR PRAYER POWER
You can hammer down any wall of Self
that separates you from God

Your scriptural strategy is as easy as **1, 2, and 3:**
1. <u>Renew</u> your mind by identifying the Self words that you have used to shut God out of your decisions and actions. <u>Explore your heart attitudes</u> that began as Self-protective measures. <u>Replace</u> Self-word motivations and actions with God-words.

2. <u>Pray out loud connecting with the Holy Spirit</u> (no intellect prayers) asking God to strengthen you and give you wisdom. <u>Confess</u> out loud your past heart motivations used in the formation of each defensive rock in your wall that keeps God at a distance.

3. **ACT!** Use God's Word as a hammer to strike effectively against every Self-word rock. Then <u>declare</u> out loud that your mind is renewed according to God's Word. <u>Declare</u> the new God-direction you have chosen

for your prayers, your thoughts, and your actions in obedience to God's Word. Finally, <u>declare</u> to God that you have removed the hindrance of your Self, that you are ready to submit to His will, and that you receive His answers in belief, no matter what they are.

KEEP GOING!!
DON'T STOP TOO SOON BEFORE COMPLETING #3

PRAISE God for that which you have declared is now a reality. **It now exists.** Continue to praise even when you don't see any prayer results. One thing God can do that no other power can do, is take His creative Book of Genesis power and speak things and beings into existence. Your prayer in agreement with God's awesome power calls things that are not as though they are. Read **Romans 4:17**

REMEMBER! You have what you say in faith believing according to God's will. Say that over and over until you believe it in your heart.

The whole process is a "spiritual make-over" empowered by the Holy Spirit. You will succeed in breaking those rocks of Self in pieces with the hammer of God's Word. Then let the abundance of unanswered prayers be released as you pray according to God's will. Your answers are no longer hindered by your Self.

Freely and wholly accept God's answers as perfect. Do not doubt! What you do not see in your limited human sight is clear to your omnipotent God. Celebrate your Holy Spirit-powered victory with praises to God. Enjoy the fruit of a new, more powerful prayer relationship with your Father, God.

This 1...2...3 pattern will serve you well when you meet with other spiritual problems. Let's recap the pattern.

1. IDENTIFY AND DEFINE THE PROBLEM. Honestly ask God to reveal to you any attitudes of the heart,

which have allowed the problem to take root in your mind and your actions.

2. PRAY, believing and connecting with Holy Spirit.

3. DESTROY PRAYER HINDRANCES by hammering them into pieces and BY DECLARING GOD'S WORD OUT LOUD. Proclaim that the deed is done by speaking your changes in actions and thoughts. No matter what you don't see or don't feel, **finish your spiritual victory with praise** and adoration of the Most High God.

Now you are ready to begin taking each area of your Self and examine how it hinders your communication with God. Destroy it, claim the victory, and praise God for answered prayers.

THE ROCK OF SELF-WILL

CAUTION! WORK THIS ROCK THROUGH CAREFULLY. Identify anything that relates to your thoughts, beliefs, or behaviors.

1. IDENTIFY THE ROCK OF SELF-WILL:
● *One's own will; a dominant act or use of power; persistence in attempts to do as one chooses; includes the power of determination of choice; to seek to force; to influence. Scripture definitions include:* <u>rebellion</u>, *stiff-necked, disobedience, transgression, resistance.*

This Rock also includes FREE WILL: *voluntary choice or decision, freedom of human beings to make choices.* God has given us free will and will not take it back. He gives us the choice between Life and Death and He says, "Therefore, choose life." We are free to make wrong, selfish choices. Life is what He wants for us, but we retain the power of our will to choose even death.

You have the power of your will to choose to believe or not. You have the power to obey or not. After you sort out what God requires of you in order to receive His promises, you have the power to choose to *submit your will to God's will--or not!* Remember picking and choosing what words and requirements of God you obey and which of these you do not obey by switching back and forth *between* God's will and your own will, is <u>double-mindedness</u>. Scripture says that when you do this, you cannot expect to receive any thing from *God including* answers to your prayers. God greatly values your faith and obedience.

Identify <u>Heart Attitudes of Self-Will</u>, either past or present. Look for hidden evidence of Self will expressed either inwardly through thoughts or spoken to others. These suggestions are to help you recall your own past thoughts and actions.

- I don't care what you do or say. I'm going to do it my way.
- My way or the highway.
- I know what's best.
- You can't make me stop; I'll do it anyway.
- Why are you doing it that way? Try this.
- You don't know what you're doing.
- Move over and let me do it right.
- I don't care what the law says; it doesn't apply to me. I'll do what I want.
- I don't like to do what people tell me to do.
- I' m not stupid. I can do things without anybody telling me how.
- Laws are made to be broken.
- I know more than you do so I'll do it my way.

How many unwise decisions have you made in your own will without God? How many unwise decisions have you made after consulting God and His Word first? Those were easy questions for me to answer. My unwise decisions were beyond counting. My success rate was in the pits, and I was NOT happy. Gradually, however, I learned to talk things over with God and trust Him by choosing to do things His way. Knowing scripture helps when you get into sticky decision-making, because His Word is His will. It is wise, true, perfect, and eternal, which is miles above and beyond what I was choosing to do.

USE A CONCORDANCE

It's easy to go to the short concordance, a kind of subject dictionary in the back of your Bible. It is *not* the index. Find out what God has to say on any given subject. Since I have been talking with God (talking is also prayer) and reading His Word, I make fewer mistakes. Some things He says I don't understand, but when I act on them, they work out great anyway. At first there were times when things got a little shaky, because I wasn't sure I heard God correctly. Ultimately, after prayer for guidance and multiple mistakes, I submitted my will to His, and I have never regretted it. I don't want His job. *I don't need to be in the driver's seat.* I'm enjoying letting Him be in control, going where He sends me and doing what He's called me to do. My only regret is that I didn't make that decision sooner.

I am out of the *Self will* groove and into the *God's will zone* now. It's your decision and your will to act as you choose. *You cannot serve two masters.* When you have a divided mind or heart, you cannot serve either master with faithfulness or integrity. You will be constantly in conflict within your Self and find it hard to prosper. You will have no real peace until you choose to be obedient to God.

2. PRAY - CONNECT WITH THE HOLY SPIRIT. Pray this prayer out loud.

Father God, You know my inmost thoughts and desires. You know me better than I know myself. I thank You, Holy Spirit, for being faithful in recalling scriptures to my mind whenever I need to make a decision. You strengthen me when I want to waver in my faithfulness to God.

Sometimes I think, "What difference can this one decision make?" not knowing the pitfalls that lie ahead. Lord, You cause me to pause and reconsider whose will is it that I'm obeying. Lord, teach me to be patient when I want to be like King Saul. He couldn't wait for You to do what You promised because he saw things falling apart around him. He deliberately disobeyed You and tried to fix things himself. It didn't work for him, and I know it won't work for me.

God, I thank You for warning me, when I impatiently want to choose my own will instead of Your perfect will. I submit my will to You and lay it on the altar as a sacrifice I want to walk in Your perfect will for me. I ask for and receive, Your forgiveness when I have prayed in Self will. How can I know all the gifts and wonders that You have created in me? How else can I know the way to walk except that You guide me with Your Holy Spirit and Your Word? Blessed be the name of the Lord. Be it unto me according to Your Word. AMEN (firm and established)

3. BREAK THE SELF-WILL ROCK WITH THE HAMMER OF GOD'S WORD.

Remember! Look for God's part and <u>underline</u> it. Look for your part and (circle) it. Declare that you are now implementing just what the scripture says.

I hammer the Self-will rock with **James 4:7.** *Submit yourselves then to God. Resist the devil and he will flee from you. Come near to God and He will come near to you. Wash your hands, you sinners, and purify your hearts you double-minded.*

2 Corinthians 10:5 *...We take captive every thought to make it obedient to Christ.*

Psalm 143:10 *Teach me to do your will for you are my God; May your good Spirit lead me on level ground.*

Mathew 26:39 Jesus submitted to the Father's will. *'Yet not as I will, but as You will.'*

Philippians 2:13 (AMP**)** [Not in your own strength] *for it is God who is all the while effectually at work in you — energizing and creating in you the power and desire — both to WILL and to work for his good pleasure and satisfaction and delight.*

DECLARATION: Declare out loud that these words of God you have read, are true for you in your life:

> **I declare that the rock of SELF-WILL is destroyed in my life and I replace it with God's Word. I submit my will to God. I no longer presume to know what is best for me. I agree with God as to His will for my life, my ministry, and my loved ones. I will one will with God, my Creator, Sustainer, and Provider. I declare: The rock of Self-will is destroyed in me by the power of the mighty name of Jesus. God, I am now free to receive any answers to prayers that were blocked by Self-will.**

YOU HAVE DESTROYED YOUR FIRST ROCK OF SELF

The **1...2...3...** pattern is an important tool to use on your own even after you have finished this study. Keep reading the scriptures out loud and praying out loud, whenever you detect Self is building

42

strength again. *It is a life-long battle.* Stay alert to sneaky Self creeping into your words, your relationships, your attitudes, and your actions. The Holy Spirit will alert you to any such deception if you ask Him to do so. This is part of the process of renewing your mind.

Until you are comfortable with this process and are able to hear the Holy Spirit within you, use the pattern as a guide. I can recall how awkward it was for me to even remember to use simple spiritual principles, because they were so new and different from my faith walk at the time. It was almost as if my intellect were fighting against the process. I would have welcomed a simple reminder or pattern to help me, so here is a condensed reminder if you need it. Always CONNECT with the Holy Spirit in Prayer and CONFESS your Self-attitude being aware of the possibility of Self-deception.

PATTERN OF MIND-RENEWAL

1. IDENTIFY the Self-Rock and explore the hidden attitudes of your heart.

2. SUBMIT your Self to God in prayer and confession.

3. BREAK each Rock with the Hammer of God's Word; then, DECLARE it done in the Power of Jesus' name. Ask God to release the prayers prayed under the influence and through ignorance of this Self-rock. **Then look for prayer answers.**

PRAYER OF PREPARATION ALWAYS COMES FIRST.
- Ask for a protective covering over you and your family.
- Ask for wisdom to discern God's will for you as you read scripture, sorting out your part from God's part.
- Pray God's will be done, not yours.

After all has been said and done comes the time of waiting where you must hold fast to your faith. Believe now that what you have declared is done according to God's Word. You don't have to feel anything. Feeling is in your body, not your spirit. Your spirit will have a sensing of peace or completeness which seems to be all over your body. Your mind will tell you that nothing has happened because it does not understand spiritual things. Do not be deceived. What you prayed and declared *did* happen. The body also does not understand spiritual things for they are processed in the spirit only. If you could see and feel spiritual things, then why would you need the faith that pleases God? Guard your heart and mind against unbelief. Move forward with Godly boldness. Do not return to your former way of depending upon your own abilities in mind and body.

Ask God first. Trust in His Word. **Proverbs 3:6-7** states, *In all your ways acknowledge Him and He will direct your paths. Do not be wise in your own eyes; fear (love) the Lord and shun evil. This will bring health to your body and nourishment to your bones.*

Do you see your part within the scriptures? Do you see God's part? Remember what you are supposed to do so that God can act. You have to initiate action; God waits for you to move *first*. If you don't act, God will not do it for you. Now that you have *acted* in agreement with God to destroy the rock of Self-will, don't let it slip out of your grasp. Be alert.

Now pray your own prayer of preparation asking God for wisdom, understanding, and guidance of the Holy Spirit. Continue on your journey to the next rock of Self-sufficiency.

THE ROCK OF
SELF-SUFFICIENCY

1. IDENTIFY THE ROCK OF SELF-SUFFICIENCY:
Requiring nothing from without; independent; unaided; individualistic; one's own man. Prefers to work alone rather than in unity with others. Refuses sincere offers of help from caring others even in simple situations, fearing to be perceived as: weak, vulnerable, unable, stupid, controllable, or needy. Takes offense to an offer of help thinking that it is criticism, a veiled judgment, which infers that what you are doing is not good enough. The focus on Self denies the loving motivations of others.

God's Word constantly reminds you of His desire for you to live together in love, to love one another, and to be in community with one another. You are not to isolate yourself from fellowship of the Body of Christ. Love draws people together, but selfishness, fear, and lies about Self-worth, pull them apart. It is a lie to think that you are Self-sufficient. From the time that you are born, you depend upon the loving care and nurturing of another. When you seek to isolate your Self from others because of wounds, disappointments, or betrayals, you cannot prosper in body, soul, or spirit. We are all ONE body in Christ. Man was not Self-sufficient from the beginning of his creation.

Genesis 2:18 says, *The Lord God said," It is not good for the man to be alone. I will make him a <u>helper</u> suitable for him…"* God's desire for us is a oneness and a completeness only satisfied by living in a loving relationship with Him and in love and unity with others.

Psalm 133:1 says, *How good and pleasant it is when brothers live together in unity.* God's word is true. Self-sufficiency is a lie and He Himself created man, Adam, to fellowship and enjoy Him forever.

In 1 John 1:3, scripture tells us: *God, who has called you into fellowship with His son Jesus Christ our Lord, is faithful.* God desires us to be in loving fellowship with the Israelites, His chosen people. It was Jesus who united us, the gentiles, with God's chosen people, the Hebrews.

Ephesians 3:6 says: *The mystery is that through the gospel the Gentiles are heirs together with Israel members of ONE BODY, and sharers together in the promise of Christ Jesus.* We are to be in loving fellowship with other believers.

1 John 1:7 (AMP) *says: But if we [really] are living and walking in the Light, as He [Himself] is in the Light, we have [true, unbroken] fellowship with one another. . .* That is God's desire for you.

Identify <u>Heart Attitudes of Self-sufficiency</u>. Look for inward thoughts and outward actions. The suggestions may help you recall your own thoughts and actions – past and present.

- I don't need anybody's help. It's easier to do it myself or let it go undone.
- They think I'm stupid and unable to do this on my own.
- I'm pretty independent. I like to handle things myself.
- I'm not lost. I can find my way. I have a map.
- If you don't like the way I'm doing it, do it yourself.
- I love to give, but it is hard for me to receive.
- Needing something means that I am weak in the eyes of others.
- I really don't <u>need</u> God.
- Don't tell me what to do.
- I don't take advice, I give it.
- I don't need anything, thank you. I say this when I really do need something, but I don't want anyone to think I am lacking in provision or ability.
- When I do things myself, I know they're done right and I'm not responsible for someone else's mistakes.

When you change Self-sufficiency to God-sufficiency, you get a renewed mind which generates unity in the body of Christ.

Humbleness opens up opportunities to confess betrayals, wounds, and disappointments to one another. Without confessing your needs, you deny yourself the comfort of God's love and the expressions of love from fellow Christians.

James 5:16 says: *Therefore confess your sins to each other and pray for each other so that you may be healed...* God supplies for all your needs. He loves you with an everlasting love and showers you with loving-kindness. He wipes tears from your eyes. The hard part is confessing your sins to each other. That makes you vulnerable to fear of betrayal. Learn to rely on the truth of God's Word.

Philippians 4:19 says: *And my God will meet all your needs according to his glorious riches in Christ Jesus.* You can depend upon God, Who does not change. He is the same yesterday, today, and tomorrow. You can depend on God – not your Self. God's undeserved favor is more than enough for all of your needs. If you have trouble believing these things, you are doubting and full of fear that God will not value you enough to fulfill His promise to you.

2 Corinthians 12:9 says: *My grace is sufficient for you, for my power is made perfect in weakness.*

When you attempt to supply for your own needs or even prepare for your future so that you lack nothing, you have Jesus' teaching of the Parable of the Rich Fool to guide you. Read **Luke 12:31.** It will show you that Self-sufficiency doesn't work in God's kingdom. This parable lesson teaches that a man's life and future do not consist in the abundance of his possessions or his comfort. Hoarding and storing up riches do not supply all your needs. It is time to switch assurance of provision in tough times from Self to God.

2. CONNECT WITH THE HOLY SPIRIT IN PRAYER

Lord God, my Provider, show me where I have any lingering Self sufficiency, any pride in my own accomplishments, or wisdom for providing for my own and my family's future. Forgive my insistence for the times when in anger and disappointment, I have said," I don't need any body or anything from any body." You, in Your great love, have cared for me even when I rejected Your help. I can see Your care in what I thought to be coincidence. Near accidents have not been luck or living right.

Jesus said, "Behold, I am with you always". Thank You, God that I don't have to be Self sufficient, for if I were, I would have been killed years ago. How many times have You rescued me, Lord?

Forgive my egotistical faith in my own Self-sufficiency. I lay it down before You and praise Your name for Your everlasting love and patience with me. Thank You for David's <u>Psalm 34.</u> Thank You for sending angels to guard me and for holding me in the palm of Your hand. I rely on Your complete love and provision. You have said in the love <u>Chapter 13 of First Corinthians</u> that everything will fail, but love will endure eternally. It says nothing about possessions. Your loving provision supplies for me completely.

I want to put this understanding into practice, God, but my faith is not there yet. Help my unbelief so I can grow in understanding and be at peace, no matter what the financial or physical circumstances.

<u>Psalm 1</u> tells me that I will be like a tree planted by the river, where I will not lack anything needed to bring forth fruit in my season, and whatever I do will prosper because of Your unfailing love. I receive all these promises. AMEN (firm and established)

3. BREAK THE ROCK OF SELF-SUFFICIENCY WITH THE HAMMER OF GOD'S WORD.

READ <u>Psalm 34</u> out loud in its entirety. As you read these power-packed words, listen and welcome the power of God's Word into your life. When you have finished, separate out what is your part and what is God's part. Then purpose in your heart to do what God requires of you. Declare those purposes out loud.

Psalm 139: 3, 5 *You hem me in behind and before; You have Your hand laid upon me. You discern my going out and my lying down. You are* *familiar with all my ways.*

Matthew 4:6 *He will command his angels concerning you and they will lift you up in their hands, so that you will not strike your foot against a stone.* This same verse appears three times in scripture. I think God wants you to "get it".

Hebrews 1:14 *Are not all ministering spirits sent to serve those who will inherit salvation?*

Psalm 91:11 *For He will command his angels concerning you to guard you in all your ways.*

Psalm 34:4,7 *I sought the Lord and he answered me; he delivered me from all my fears. The angel of the Lord encamps around those who fear him and he delivers them.*

DECLARE: God's Word is true. His grace (unmerited favor) is enough for me. He is God, and I am a sheep of His pasture and in His loving care. There is no way I was, or ever could be, Self-sufficient. I reject the concept of Self-sufficiency as a lie and look to my loving Lord God for all my needs. I will no longer think of my Self as able to do anything without Jesus, who said, "Apart from me you can do nothing," I believe that Jesus is the vine and that I am a branch. I choose to remain in Him and He will remain in me. I will bear much fruit. (paraphrase of **John 15:5**)

PRAY: *I now thank You, God that through the power of Your Holy Word, the Self-sufficient prayer block is destroyed. And now, O Lord, I ask You to release those answers held back because of my attitudes of Self sufficiency, unbelief, and my unwillingness to receive those answers. Blessed be the Name of the Lord. AMEN* (firm and established)

THE ROCK OF
SELF-CONFIDENCE

1. IDENTIFY THE ROCK OF SELF-CONFIDENCE: *Secure, fearless, self-collected, poised, and* <u>*confident in one's own ability;*</u> *self-assured, self-dependent.* An over-abundance of self-confidence becomes arrogance and pride. A balanced self-confidence is expressed in poised, self-collected, secure behavior. Lack of self-confidence is expressed through fearful behavior and feelings of unworthiness.

Paul said in **Romans 12:3,** *Do not think of yourselves more highly than you ought, but rather think of yourself with sober judgment in accordance with the measure of faith God has given you.*

Identify <u>Heart-Attitudes of your present or past</u> which express any negative form of Self-confidence. Do any of these attitudes fit you? All of these suggestions may not apply to you, but they can act as triggers to identify your own personal thoughts and inner feelings.

- Why didn't they ask me to do that? I can do it better than he can.
- I don't need any help. I got it taken care of.
- I need to volunteer to do it to be sure that the job gets done.
- Even if someone asked me to do this, I'd have to say no because I'm not as good as they think I am. I will probably fail. I don't want to be criticized.
- I'm the only one who can really do this job right.
- I can't depend upon anyone but myself. People let me down.
- I have to do everything for myself if I want it done right. My reputation depends on it.

Confidence is a necessary attribute for all people, but the *source* of the confidence is what makes the difference. The world sees confidence differently than God does. When you are <u>Self-confident,</u> you must depend upon your own resources of wisdom, physical and mental abilities. Judgments and prejudices formed by both positive and negative life experiences, color your emotional strength and character.

When you are God-confident, you recognize that you are a child of God, therefore depend upon God's resources and *His perfect will* for your life. Living in obedience to God's Word gives you unlimited confidence and security regardless of your life experiences. A good Bible verse to remember when you lack confidence is **Philippians 4:13:** *I can do everything through him (Jesus) who gives me strength.*

John 5:30 Jesus said: *By myself I can do nothing.* When you follow Jesus' example with confidence, you are empowered by God, not your own abilities. Change from Self-confident to God-Confident.

2. CONNECT WITH THE HOLY SPIRIT IN PRAYER:

My God and my Strength, I give You permission to become my confidence – that I may speak and act boldly. I lay down confidence in my Self and I receive Your perfect confidence. I rely on Your wisdom and teaching. I want my actions and words before men to be acceptable in Your sight. I know that Jesus lives in me so that I can do all things for Your glory through Him who strengthens me. I now choose to receive God-confidence in every area of my life. I believe that Your power to give me confidence is stronger than my doubts and fears. Help me to walk confidently in this world as a child of God These words are firm and established by the power of Jesus' name. AMEN

Believe and do not doubt that God has done just as you have prayed because He promises to give you whatever you ask in His will. You have just asked according to His will.

USE THIS HAMMER TO BREAK
SELF-EMPOWERED CONFIDENCE:

*'Is not my word like a fire,' declares the Lord, 'and like a
hammer that breaks a rock in pieces?'*
Jeremiah 23: 29

3. BREAK CONFIDENCE IN SELF WITH THE HAMMER OF GOD'S WORD

Break the Self-confidence rock with God's Word which is your Hammer. Become confident in yourself as the servant God made you to be. Trust His word and His promises. Stop Self-centered, defensive behaviors resulting in fearful avoidance of loving personal relationships. God will guide you. Read **Psalm 139** entirely to gain understanding of who God made you to be.

Psalm 139:13,14 *For you created my inmost being, you knit me together in my mother's womb, I praise you because I am fearfully and wonderfully made. I cannot begin to comprehend this creature you have fashioned [me to be], I can only look upon him with awe and wonder. Your works are wonderful* (notes from NIV Study Bible).

Discover the Truth of who God made you to be. You don't have to become over-confident in order to convince others of your value. Do not be content with believing the Self-image (the one *you* formed, not God) the world around you has molded and controlled through ungodly influences. The truth is who God has said that you are. What the world, your relatives, an over-active ego, or circumstances say you are, *is not the truth.*

Read the following scriptures out loud, because God says *Faith comes by hearing and hearing comes by hearing the Word of God.* Don't forget to look for your part and God's part. <u>Underline</u> God's part and (circle) your part.

1 John 5:14, 15 *This is the confidence we have in approaching God: that if we ask anything according to His will, He hears us.* If we know that He hears us—whatever we ask according to His will—we know that we *have* what we asked of Him.

Proverbs 3:26 *For the Lord will be your confidence and will keep your foot from being snared.* Trust in God's promise to be your confidence. Use His confidence, not yours.

Proverbs 3:5,6 *Trust in the Lord with all your heart and lean not on your own understanding; in all your ways acknowledge him and he will make your paths straight.*

DECLARE: (Speak out loud *in belief*)
> **I no longer gain confidence from my Self, but from God. I walk in God-confidence. I will not be Self-deceived any longer by leaning on my own understanding. My confidence is in God alone. With the hammer of God's word, I have broken the hindrance of Self-generated confidence into pieces, and I replace it with my confidence in God, and God's confidence in me.**

PRAY: *Lord, I ask You to forgive me for my double-mindedness when I say that I trust You but continue to act with confidence in my Self. I think that I know what You must do to help me and ask for that kind of help. I have been guilty of telling You how to answer my prayers and as a result, these prayer answers have been hindered by my sinful focus on Self. Lord, I ask Your forgiveness. I, now, expectantly receive Your wisdom and Your power to pray according to Your will and Your plan as You direct me. I thank You, God, that I can now walk in God-confidence. Through the power of Your Holy Word, I destroy the hindrance of the Self rock , and, by faith, I receive Your confidence to live my life relying upon You. AMEN* (firm and established)

 *Evaluate where you are at this point.*

If you are spiritually tired, take a break. What you are doing is intense! It may take a span of time before you can completely absorb what you have learned, prayed, and declared. You have finished the first three of the twelve self-rocks contained in this Book 1. The same pattern is continued throughout the remaining rocks.

1) Identify the rock. **2)** Pray. **3)** Break the rock with God's Word and declare your changes. You will be tearing down the Self wall which you have built over the years. You will continue to break every rock in pieces until you are no longer separated from God by the wall of Self. Then, look for and welcome your answers to prayer.

TAKE YOUR TIME

- If you need more prayer and meditation on God's Word before leaving this Rock of Self-Confidence, don't be rushed. Go back over some things that stood out or hit home. Commit important scriptures to memory, write them on note cards and post or record them in a notebook for future reference. Make them accessible. If they are hard to find when you need them, you will have yielded your Self to the powerlessness of defeat. You cannot defeat Self alone. You need God's powerful Word to do it.

Record your chosen scriptures now on sticky notes, index cards, a notebook etc.

- As you continue your journey, when you complete the destruction of a Self rock, write your scripture weapon on a separate card or in a notebook. I know from experience that you will not go back and hunt for it again. When you need a scripture weapon, you need it *immediately. There will be* no time to look it up in this book. I still have my original chosen scriptures and continue to use them if I forget where they are in the Bible or the details of what they say. I can usually remember pieces, but not the entire verse which is usually the part that I really need.

RENEW YOUR MIND

- Take your time and be as completely free of each Rock as you can now discern. You will have peace in your spirit. By now you may be beginning to recognize it. If not, keep trying. The recognition will come. This is not something you can finish in a short period of time. Remember you are renewing your mind in a deep way. You are spiritually changing the way that you see the world. You are moving from focus on Self to focus on God so that you are no longer hindered in receiving God's answers to prayer.

PRAY EFFECTIVELY

- It is important to have a sense of calmness, peace or completeness when you have finished with a Self rock. If you don't experience this, go back and read aloud the prayers and scriptures again.

- PRAY until you spiritually sense that you have completed what you have set out to do with each rock. You will sense a kind of release, a peace - not doubt, tension, or uneasiness in your spirit.

- Mark anything that will require a return visit because your spirit is sensing that the work on this rock is not yet complete.

OPTIONS FOR WHEN YOU BEGIN AGAIN

1. Remember! When you begin again you have to break each rock individually. You may determine your own order if you wish, but do not omit any Self rock. You may be surprised what the Holy Spirit *reveals* to you in an area where you think that there is nothing that needs to be addressed. How are you going

to know that it is the Holy Spirit? The idea may just pop into your head totally unrelated to what you were thinking. You may get one of those "light-bulb-over-the-head" moments.

2. You may wish to select only the Self rocks you feel confident you can deal with now. Save the toughies until last when you have gained more spiritual understanding. Allow extra time for rocks that seem difficult to break. Leave Self-Centeredness until the end.

3. Take time to concentrate on your prayer. You may be praying each one more than once until you spiritually sense a peace that what you have prayed is truly your own desire before God. Make changes and additions to the prayers as the Holy Spirit reveals personal things to you.

4. If any scripture seems particularly meaningful to you, it may be God speaking directly to you from His Word. Make a sticky note or 3 x 5 card copy of it, and place God's Word where you can see it often in order to memorize and meditate on it. When you sense a particular strength, emphasis, excitement of a scripture, pay attention!

5. I suggest that you make a sort of diary of what you are sensing spiritually on each Self rock as you go. It will help to crystallize your thinking. When you are finished with this journey from Self to God, if you doubt that any particular rock was destroyed, your diary notes will be evidence of your spiritual victories. You cannot be robbed of what God has done through your prayers and declarations. Your ego will be the first to lie to you and tell you that:

- Nothing has changed.
- God didn't do anything.
- You have not changed.
- You cannot change.
- This rock breaking with scripture is not working for you. You didn't *feel* any change.

If that happens, you can refer to your diary notes to refresh your memory and refuse to be deceived into losing what you have spiritually won through submitting your Self to God.

6. Be sure to confess what you see you have been doing wrong and ask for forgiveness. Thank God and praise Him for your victory over Self and for leading and sustaining you through this process. When you finish, not only will you experience a new freedom in prayer, but you will be able to tell someone else how to do the same thing.

Remember! Don't skip any rocks. Even if you don't think that a particular rock applies to you, it may identify some one you know. It may provide you with a direction on how to pray and intercede for that person.

THE ROCK OF
SELF-RESPECT

1. IDENTIFY THE ROCK OF SELF-RESPECT: *Dignity, pride, self-assurance, self-confidence, integrity, honesty, and good reputation.* It includes your Self image built upon inner qualities molded by people (usually family) and circumstances. Self-respect is also built upon how people nurture, respond, and relate to you. Respect of Self grows from the value others place upon you as a person, recognizing within you the same qualities and character traits that the world acknowledges as admirable.

Respect is synonymous with honor and value. It is tied in meaning to admiration, esteem, appreciation, regard, veneration, and reverence. In times past honor was a vital part of a family name. You needed a good, honest name to do business because your reputation was of vital importance; today honor has taken a back-seat to the influence of wealth and power. Children are taught by the media to DIS-respect parents and authority figures portraying them as stupid, over-bearing, and tyrannical. It appeals to a sense of helplessness and rebelliousness. They are also entertained by movie and cartoon children who have power over adults through magic spells, witchcraft, deception, and manipulation. If there is no mutual respect shared among family members, then domination and control are the foundation for relationships. Parents who respect their children and teach them honor, will be respected. How can children know what respect is unless they receive it and see parents respecting each other?

Identify <u>Heart Attitudes of Dis-respect for Self,</u> expressed either by inward thoughts or outward actions.

- I don't respect who I am. I just don't fit other people's expectations.
- I don't feel worthy.
- I don't like to speak to people making direct eye contact. They make me extremely uncomfortable.
- I walk avoiding looking at the people that I pass.
- I leave a big space when taking a seat in a church or at a ball game, in a doctor's office; I will not sit next to someone.
- I do not expect to be respected nor have my opinions considered.
- I get no respect, and I ask for none for I do not respect my Self.
- I do not honor and respect others. They have to earn respect from me-- especially if they demand my respect.
- I would appreciate a respectful attitude towards me, but I know it won't happen.
- I have to work hard to earn respect.
- I am owed respect regardless of my actions.
- I respect others who don't respect me.
- I am not respected by my boss or others in authority over me.
- I feel like a second-class citizen without hope of consideration or recognition.
- I do not respect authority. It is not fair to me.
- I measure my value according to the respect I get from my family and others.
- Those who are older or younger have prejudices concerning my age, physical appearance or health. They do not respect what I can do or who I am.
- Lack of respect for me is based on my race, financial status, social status, or my Christian beliefs.

DECLARE: I declare here and now that I change my attitude of Self respect and re-direct it to *God respect* which gives me favor and unconditional love. I do not rely on the ever-changing respect of others. I am able to respect my Self, because God created me according to His perfect

plan. God does not give me favor because of my worldly accomplishments but because He created me to be <u>exactly</u> who I am. Those who do not respect me either do not know God, or they do not know God's plan for my life. I choose to agree with God Whose plan for me is perfect regardless of how others see me.

You have God's respect. He places a high value on you. **Leviticus 26:3,9** *If you follow my decrees and are careful to obey my commands...I will look on you with favor and make you fruitful and increase your numbers and I will keep my covenant with you. Look on you with favor* is also translated 'have respect unto you.'] Because God looks on you with favor, you have all the respect you *need*. Respect from the world involves pride. God's favor is better by far. Respect the Holy Spirit in you and the truth of God's Word written on your heart. There is no need for you to have worldly respect before you can respect your Self or receive respect from God.

2. CONNECT WITH THE HOLY SPIRIT IN PRAYER
PRAY:

Lord, how long I have desired respect from those around me in the world of work. I had a desire for recognition so that I could respect my Self. I thought my true value depended upon how others honored me and how others showed me favor. My family didn't count because "They gotta love me".

How discontent and frustrated I am when I set my sights on the lower worldly honors bestowed by people. You have already called me to a higher, spiritual purpose planted within me from before the time I was knit together in my mother's womb. When I respect and honor You with my praise and adoration, I have no need of basing my value upon the fleeting respect that the world gives.

Thank You, God, that I never received that once-coveted respect else I would not have sought You. I would have been satisfied with the temporary, trivial approval and stopped searching missing all that You have planned for me. I don't have to earn respect. You are no respecter of persons. No one receives favoritism from You as the world sees favoritism. What You have done for anyone else, You will do for me. All who love and obey You receive the same promises, prosperity, and favor equally as Your child. There is no need for worldly position. It is empty of meaning unless You have placed me in that position. Sometimes worldly respect contains a few empty words of praise or a plaque to hang on the wall. When I respect and honor You with my praise and adoration, I have no need for the things that do not satisfy. I know that You will place me in whatever worldly position You have planned for me to serve You best. I want people to see Jesus in me. **You** *supply for all my needs, not my place of employment. You alone bestow all the favor and honor that I will ever want or need. I am a child of the Most High God.*

Thank You, God, for being patient with me and waiting for me to seek respect and honor from You. I give You complete control of my life. It is my joy to serve You, my Strength and my Redeemer. AMEN (firm and established)

3.
● BREAK THE ROCK OF SELF-RESPECT WITH THE HAMMER OF GOD'S WORD. The following scriptures are words of respect and integrity. Memorize the starred ones .

Acts 10:34 (AMP) *And Peter opened his mouth and said, "Most certainly and thoroughly now I perceive and understand that God shows no partiality and is no respecter of person".*

***Psalm 84:11.12 *For the Lord God is a sun and shield; the Lord bestows favor and honor; no good thing does He withhold from those that walk blamelessly. O Lord Almighty, blessed is the man who trusts in you.*

Romans 2:11 *For God does not show favoritism.* Neither did Jesus and neither should you.

Ephesians 6:1-3 *Children, obey your parents in the Lord, for this is right; "Honor your father and mother" – which is the first* *commandment with a promise – "that it may go well with you and that you may enjoy long life on the earth."*

Psalms 15:1-5 *Lord, who may dwell in your sanctuary? Who may live on your holy hill? He whose walk is blameless and who does what is righteous, Who speaks the truth from his heart and has no slander in his tongue, who does his neighbor no wrong. And casts no slur on his fellow man, who despises a vile man but honors those who fear the Lord, who keeps his oath even when it hurts, Who lends his money without usury and does not accept a bribe against the innocent. He who does these things will never be shaken.*

These scriptures are God's idea of integrity, honor and respect. If you are being obedient to God's Word, you <u>have</u> respect, honor, and integrity whether or not the world agrees.   If any person shows you disrespect, that person is a liar and a deceiver. He does not speak the truth of God. God's Word <u>is</u> true--forever.

Romans 2:10 *But glory, honor, and peace for everyone who does good: first for the Jew and then for the Gentile.*

Colossians 3:25 (AMP) *For he who deals wrongfully will reap the fruit of his folly and there is no partiality [no matter what a person's position may be] whether he is the slave or the master.*

***Luke 22:37 *It is written, "And he was numbered with the transgressors".* Jesus received no respect from the worldly system. It opposed him and his teachings.   He was crucified with thieves.
See also   **James 2:1-8; 1 Samuel 2:30; 1 Peter 1:17**

DECLARE: I declare that I respect, honor, love and worship my God above all created things. I declare that my hope is in God and His everlasting love for me. I do not seek the favor of worldly honors for true honor and glory are gifts of God. My Self respect is grounded in the knowledge of who God made me to be. I will not seek for empty recognition, but to walk humbly with God in obedience to whatever He has prepared for me to do.

I would rather find fulfillment being a servant in the house of my God than to share in the lives of those who do not honor God. (Psalm 84:10 paraphrased)

I do not look to my Self for respect but to God who honors me with grace and favor. I declare that the rock of Self respect which has separated me from God and blocked answers to my prayers, is broken in pieces by His Word. My mind is now renewed with God's Truth.

THE ROCK OF
SELF-CONSCIOUSNESS

1. IDENTIFY THE ROCK OF SELF CONSCIOUSNESS: *Awkward, bashful, embarrassed, ill at ease, insecure, nervous, uncomfortable. Conscious of one's own mind and its acts; conscious of being observed by others; a lover of self. A concentrating on outward appearances.* Those who are conscious of Self show Self-love, fear and a desire for comfort and protection in their innermost being.

When you become God-conscious and meditate on His word, fear and Self-consciousness fade. God's Word is more powerful than <u>any</u> fear. **2 Timothy 1:7** says, *God has not given you a spirit of fear but of power, and love, and a sound mind.* To believe otherwise is to be deceived. This is an excellent scripture to memorize and call to mind when you experience the insecure feelings listed above. Identify <u>Heart Attitudes of Self-Consciousness</u>. Look for evidence of Self-consciousness in your thoughts, your spoken words, or actions. When you sense that a particular attitude is one you have experienced, declare out loud something like, 1) That's not me any more, 2) I am changed and no longer accept that attitude, 3) <u>I refuse</u> to act in this Self-conscious manner ever again, 4) My God will help me to overcome this attitude.

- I don't like being the center of attention because people look at me and judge me.
- I don't like looking in a mirror because I have to judge myself, my hair, my body size and shape.
- I quickly make a joke of my appearance, or my actions so that others will not be able to speak words of judgment because I said what they were thinking first.
- Being in front of people makes me nervous. I don't know what they will think of me or say later behind my back.

- I dress the way I do because I don't want to draw attention to myself in any way.
- I avoid crowds and speaking to people I don't know.
- I don't know what to say to people. Sometimes I stutter or say stupid things that I don't mean to say. I even say things that don't make sense.
- I think about my Self and my feelings a lot.
- Every time someone is angry, I think that they're angry at me even if I didn't do anything to provoke the anger.
- When I compare my Self to others, I find that I get very unhappy with who I am, what I look like, and how intelligent I am. I would rather be like someone smarter, more attractive or popular.

THE FRUIT OF SELF-CONSCIOUSNESS

The world of a Self conscious Christian is so very small. It is a Self-made box used for defense against fear. Fear is a prison that does not lock out hurt, betrayal, and disappointment as much as it hems you in with fear as your only companion. There is no room for God in your life or in your tiny box-world. You can't see Jesus when you're looking at your Self and scanning the horizon for anything that might cause you pain. You are expecting to identify rejection and judgment so that you can quickly dodge it before it reaches you. Have you ever seen someone you know before they see you and you avoid an encounter by turning and going another way? Self-conscious thought patterns originate in fear and are intensified by wounds, failures, intimidations, and control by others whom you perceive to have negative opinions of you. Those patterns will disappear when you learn who God made you to be both spiritually and naturally.

If you know that you are brother, sister, and friend to your Savior, Jesus, then you have a rich and powerful inheritance. You need not – no! must not - bow down or submit to any person but your Lord and Savior. Bowing to Self consciousness is nothing but fear. It says that you believe that fear is stronger than God, your Creator. You know that's a lie, but somehow you never quite act on the truth. Old habits and false beliefs die hard! But they *do* die when faced with the truth of God's Word. **James 1:2:** *Consider it pure joy, my brothers, whenever you face trials of many kinds, because you know that the testing of your faith develops perseverance.* Your faith is tested whenever you fear because fear is doubt and unbelief - the opposite of faith in God's promises to you.

PRAY: *God, You didn't give me fear. I will not keep it and protect it. Your perfect love casts out all my fear. Fear, get out of my emotions, my thoughts, and my life – now! You will no longer deceive and torment me. **Psalm 27:1** says "The Lord is my light and my salvation-- whom shall I fear?" Lord, teach me to be God-conscious so that I will grow in power and authority, ignoring any occasion for fear. You are my Strength, my Shield, my Provider, and my Father who loves me with an ever-lasting love. I believe and pray **Psalm 73:26** to You, God. My flesh and my heart may fail, but You are the strength of my heart and my portion forever. Lord, help me to stand up straight as a confident Christian. I want to be able to look people in the eye and tell them the truth of Your provision for me. I desire the holy boldness I need to do the things which You have assigned to me. When my flesh fails, I sweat and my knees shake, I will speak Your word for my life. When my heart fails within me and I am overcome with fear of the judgment of others, I will look to You, for You uphold me with Your strong right arm. I will stand in Your courage, for I am Your child and brother to Jesus. I have a divine destiny. I am called to serve You. You make Your servants the head and not the tail. My confidence is in You. Thank You for Your words of truth and encouragement that I have claimed for my new life-focus. AMEN,* (firm and established)

BREAKING FEAR HABITS WITH
TRUTH AND TRUST

There was once a TV game show years ago called "Who Do You Trust?" Famous panelists had to guess which of the guests in the lineup were lying and which were telling the truth. They had to correctly identify the one telling the truth. It was only an entertaining game, but you are in a real life game with real spiritual consequences for guessing wrong. Where spiritual things are concerned, you don't have to guess. You have the truth of the Bible in your hands to use as a guide. But-- if you don't read it, believe it, and hide it in your heart, you are easily deceived into believing lies about your Self. There is no other truth except God's Word. That is the only trustworthy standard for identifying truth.

Sometimes it may seem to you that others are more knowledgeable because they possess worldly education, position, authority, experience, or a professional reputation. Trusting them over your own judgment is natural when you believe you have no other source of confidence except your Self. God's Word *is* your confidence. You either believe the Bible or you don't. You can't believe what it says if you don't know what's in it. The Bible is your first and only source of the truth. Without a *reliable, proven source* of truth, you will be easily deceived and backed into a box with fear where you will pull the lid down over your own head. That can happen unless you understand that when people judge you, they are only expressing an opinion, not the truth. When they tell you who you are or how good or bad you are at something, that is only their opinion. If you experience Self-consciousness, guess who is your worst critic? YOU, your SELF! Oddly enough, if you believe and act on the belief that you are inferior, you are in fact training people to treat you that way. Stand up! Look up! Walk with the confidence that you are the child of the Living God. People will treat you that way.

HOW DO YOU FIND THE TRUTH ABOUT YOUR SELF?

Jesus said, "You shall know the truth and the truth will set you free." Read the book! Learn who you really are. Find out who you are in your Christian heritage. Be free in God's truth to be who He has made you to be. If you believe lies of people who have only opinions, you are a prisoner of their lies. You can never fulfill God's purpose for your life because you don't believe who scripture says you are. Remember the catch phrase for kids a few years ago: "God Doesn't Make Junk"? That's still true today for any age. God is your Creator and whatever God has made is good! No one can know you, your talents, your potential, and most important of all, your heart, the way God knows you. God is the only source of truth about your Self. Ask Him to reveal that truth to you.

2. CONNECT WITH THE HOLY SPIRIT IN PRAYER

Father, I understand now that I focus on my Self because I have fear of people, a fear of being rejected and criticized. You have not given me that spirit of fear. You have given me the Holy Spirit to teach me and lead me into all truth. Lead me, Lord, into the truth about my Self that I might not fear how others see and relate to me. Help me to focus on You and Your Word, so that I may learn to see the person You created me to be, not who others say that I am. Lord, I often give control of what I do to others because I fear that I don't know enough or may say something wrong. I fear to be judged and rejected by those I consider better than I am. I long to be free of judgment. Jesus does not condemn me, He came to lead me into righteousness and to have life to the full. Teach me who I am in Jesus. Teach me how to hide Your Word in my heart that I may not sin against You. I now understand that in making my Self the focus of my thoughts I have fallen into a trap of deception. I ask for Your forgiveness and receive Your unconditional love. Jesus draws me to him with ever-lasting love: He does not condemn me. Because my Savior does not condemn me, neither do I any longer judge or condemn my Self. I will not accept condemnation and lack of respect from others. I am Your child and I desire for You to delight in me.

Lead me in Your paths, O God, and teach me Your ways that I may become who You have created me to be. I give You complete control and I am now free to choose to serve You, my loving Father, not my fearful Self. AMEN (I believe what I just prayed).

3. BREAK THE ROCK OF SELF-CONSCIOUSNESS WITH THE HAMMER OF GOD'S WORD.

Don't forget to <u>underline</u> God's job and (circle) your job.

There are two helpful angles for the breaking of this rock. 1) How to shake off being Self-conscious, knowing that when you're thinking (meditating on God and His Word) you cannot be afraid at the same time. 2) How to put on God-consciousness. Know that God's Word is stronger than your fear.

SCRIPTURE REFERENCES FOR BREAKING OFF SELF-CONSCIOUSNESS:

Proverbs 29:25 *Fear of man will prove to be a snare, but whoever trusts in the Lord is kept safe.* Memorize this verse. Speak it out loud often until you believe it with all your heart, and you will never fear the condemnation of people again. You will be free.

Proverbs 23:7 *As a man thinks in his heart, so is he...* If you think that you are powerless and rejected, you will act that way. If you know that you are loved, accepted by God, with talents, gifts, and a spiritual destiny, then you will indeed act in that way. Seek God and ask Him to reveal your gifts and your destiny.

Philippians 4:8 *Finally, brothers, whatever is true, whatever is noble, whatever is right, whatever is pure, whatever is lovely, whatever is admirable, if anything is excellent or praiseworthy--think about such things.* If you are thinking as God commands, you will have no room or time left over for negative thoughts of Self-consciousness.

P – PLANTER MEMORY KEY FOR
PHILIPPIANS 4:8

I could never remember the "whatever's" in the above scripture so I made an acronym to help me. P-PLANTER---<u>P</u>ure-<u>P</u>raiseworthy-<u>L</u>ovely-<u>A</u>dmirable-<u>N</u>oble-<u>T</u>rue-<u>E</u>xcellent-<u>R</u>ight. By the time I think through my memory key, I have forgotten the ungodly Self conscious things that I did not want to think about in the first place. It works for me. Find what works for you. Note: other translations will have a different but similar list which might be easier for you to remember.

Psalm 119:11 *I have hidden Your Word in my heart that I might not sin against you.*

2 Timothy 1:7 *God has not given us a spirit of fear but of power and love and a sound mind.*

See also: **Psalm 19:14 and   Psalm 1:2,3**

Go from here to declaring freedom from fear, which is the root of Self consciousness.

SCRIPTURE REFERENCES FOR PUTTING ON GOD-CONSCIOUSNESS:

Psalm 119:15 *I meditate on your precepts and consider your ways.*

Psalm 63:6-8 *On my bed I remember You; I think of You through the watches of the night. Because You are my help, I sing in the shadow of Your wings. My soul clings to You; Your right hand upholds me.* This is an excellent scripture to memorize.   Paul said that he did not fear what man could do to him. He stood in faith, trusting God. He even sang God's praises while in prison.   SING AND CLING, as the scriptures indicate, when you begin to fear man. Walk boldly, confident in the knowledge that you are loved and empowered of your loving Creator.   Praise Him in song.   Meditate on His goodness.

Psalm 104:34 *May my meditation be pleasing to him, as I rejoice in the Lord.* **Philippians 4:4** *Rejoice in the Lord always. I will say it again. Rejoice!* There is no place for negativity in Joy and Praise.   When your brooding thoughts head into a downward spiral---SING in the shadow of God's wings, and CLING to God whose right hand is holding you up.

DECLARE: Fear, I am a child of God. Self-consciousness, you don't belong in my life. How can I spread the Good News as Jesus commands me when you try to keep me from even speaking to those who don't know Jesus? You want to keep me from obeying God. Get out of my life in every area, stay out. I will not allow you to torment me any longer in the name of my Lord and Savior, Jesus the anointed Son of God.

Thank you, God, for hearing my words and answering my prayer. I declare that according to God's Word, *my fear is gone*. I gladly exchange my Self-consciousness for God consciousness. I exchange my weakness for God's strength.

RENOUNCE your old view of your Self and receive the truth of God. Declare these words out loud in strong belief:

I break the rock of Self-consciousness and receive God consciousness and confidence in its place. I believe the truth of who God says that I am. I am a victor — 1 Corinthians 15:55; His ambassador — 2 Corinthians 5:20; a child of God — John 13:33; a conqueror — Romans 8:37; worthy because of Jesus — 2 Thessalonians 1:5. I stand on the truth of God's Word.

I tear up my box which has served as my past protection against fear. I serve God now, not the ever-changing whims of those who would dominate and control me with fear. I will no longer seek to protect my Self. I will keep my eyes on Jesus, not on Self. I am renewing my mind with the power of the Word of God. I will not back up or retreat into a Self-conscious box ever again! I am free to follow Jesus and to proclaim His mighty works to unbelievers through word and example. I worship and serve my Heavenly Father.

And furthermore, I declare: God doesn't make junk-- Whatever He has made is perfect. I was made in His image, and from this time forward I will act like the child of a king. Jesus is my brother and He has called me friend. Anyone who speaks otherwise to me I will ignore because I now understand who I am and the truth of my Christian heritage. Those who judge me, break the command of God Who has said, "Judge not that you be not judged". I will stand before people without fear for I have received the gifts of God in my life and I reject fear because it is the opposite of faith. I know now that without faith I cannot please God. I refuse to please people out of fear. In the name of my Savior, Jesus, I declare that Self-consciousness no longer hinders my prayers. I have destroyed it with the hammer of God's Word.

THE ROCK OF
SELF-CONDEMNATION

1. IDENTIFY THE ROCK OF SELF-CONDEMNATION: • This is another form of self-focus or conceit. The concept of condemning one's Self is contrary to God's Word. *Condemnation is judgment, Self-blame, Self-censure; to pronounce one's Self to be guilty or inadequate.* Self-condemnation is toxic to followers of Jesus because Jesus, Himself, said in **Matthew 7:1-2**, *Do not judge, or you too will be judged. For in the same way you judge others, you will be judged.* This is not an option; it is a command with a consequence for disobedience. **Acts 10:42** explains, *He [Jesus] is the one whom God appointed as judge of the living and the dead.* You have *not* been given the authority to judge others nor to judge your Self. Condemnation is only one part of an empty well of soul-stealing efforts to defeat God's purpose in your life.

THE SELF CONDEMNATION CYCLE LEADS TO SPIRITUAL PARALYSIS

In the process of condemning of your Self – which you now realize is against God's word - you accelerate a toxic cycle that is already in the process of leading you away from God and into *spiritual paralysis.* You allowed this cycle to begin when you *accepted* criticism as fact – not just opinion. Criticism is often based upon someone else's problems – not *truth.* No matter what people say, criticism is meant to demean you, to steal your God-given destiny, and to crush your spirit. Love, not criticism, is God's way. He gives knowledge, and empowers you to grow in body, soul, and spirit. You will learn God's Truth of who you are. When you believe the words and actions of any Self-appointed authority, you are placing your intrinsic value within the manipulating hands of a liar. If ignorance of God's word allowed you to be so deceived, then, now that you are aware of the deception, you can stop the cycle with

God's Eternal Truth and be empowered by His Word to change your life from victim to victor.

BEWARE THE FEARSOME FOUR FOOTSTEPS!

In Four Fearsome Footsteps you can find your Self alienated - distanced from God. Step one – Criticism, Step two – Perfectionism, Step three - Judgment and Condemnation, Step four - Division and Alienation.

The entire process begins with <u>Criticism</u>, then gradually morphs into <u>Perfectionism</u> and unrealistic expectations of Self. You begin to judge your Self holding to an unrealistic perfect standard in order to avoid being criticized or rejected by others. If you do a perfect job, what's to criticize? Perfectionism becomes a two-edged sword. In order to avoid doing something that you cannot accomplish perfectly, you never begin projects that you can do well. Scripture tells you to do everything, even menial tasks, as unto the Lord. Your job is to please God and not to satisfy unrealistic Self-imposed standards of perfection. Next, Perfectionism solidifies into <u>Judgment</u> of Self or others. This is where a fear of God's judgment comes in. When you stop trusting in God to help you, you isolate your Self having already judged your Self to be unworthy of His love. Finally, the entire process ends in <u>Defensive Division and Alienation</u> from God and people, avoiding all possible situations in which you may be criticized. Instead of drawing near to God as He commands, you move away from Him into fearful paralysis with no hope of ever pleasing God or anyone else.

End this process NOW! Pray the following prayer to free your Self from past deceptions. *Move from pleasing Self and man to pleasing God.*

PRAY: *Lord, I have lived too long with feelings of Self-condemnation and inadequacy based upon what people have said to me and about me. They are not acting in the truth of Your Word. Even those in authority with worldly knowledge cannot know what You have created for me to be and for me to accomplish. They judge with worldly standards and not Your eternal Word. I have believed lies about my Self, who I am, what I am able to do, who You have destined me to become. These lies are or were, based upon what no one can know except You, my Creator. I look to You, my God, for truth, direction, power, knowledge, and wisdom, for You supply for all my needs and hold my destiny in Your hands.*

Lord, I ask forgiveness for believing lies instead of Your Word. I thank You for Your forgiveness. Now I am free to trust You, who You say that I am, and Your destiny for me. I give up these lies to You. Please help me to root out the false beliefs that I have accepted from my childhood past, from my memories of painful situations, and from my present thoughts. Lord, I give You my soul and spirit to cleanse completely from the paralyzing cycle of Criticism, Perfectionism, Condemnation and Alienation. Please recall to my mind Your word with which I may compare every thought about my Self. I choose to please You and You only. AMEN (firm and established)

Now that you know the truth of God's Word and have given Him permission to warn you when you are allowing the Fearsome Four to creep back into your life, you need no longer judge your Self or feel guilty for any reason. Salvation and judgment belong to Jesus. There is no need to apologize for something you had nothing to do with. In your past, you accepted guilt that was not yours. Make a decision to no longer accept judgment that no one but God has the right to make. You need no longer assume guilt, ineptness, and unworthiness because some one has accused you. You will no longer be fooled into thinking that you are guilty of causing someone's anger and frustration when the cause originates within the person himself. You will realize that you just happen to be there as an available target for the anger. You probably remember a time in childhood when stressed adults shouted, argued, or spoke harshly to you and you didn't understand why. As a spirit-led adult, you no longer assume guilt or remain silent under false accusations in order to placate an angry person. Choose to no longer employ ineffective stop-gap measures to keep peace in the family and to keep the boat from rocking. You now know, without doubt that those who condemn or point the finger of accusation are out of God's will. Model God's will for them. You represent God. Speak for Him where and when He urges you to speak a word in love to build up, not tear down.

REPRESENTING GOD'S LOVE IN CONFLICTS

Self condemnation is <u>not</u> the solution for ending conflict. It only encourages and agrees with the falsehood which you have silently accepted as true. Ignoring the anger problem doesn't work either. Hoping it will go away doesn't work. Avoiding it doesn't work. Accepting blame doesn't work. Pretending it's not happening doesn't work. Confrontation at the time doesn't work. Even rightfully defending your Self doesn't work because there is no rational thinking going on. The cause is still there, alive and well with free reign to condemn you again and again. The angry party has discovered a way to get what he wants through intimidation and domination. Love, not guilt and fear, has to be the motivation for resolving such problems.

Love is not intimidated. There is nothing stronger than love. God is love So -- while the anger is being vented, remember **Psalm 91** which says, *Because He loves me,...I will rescue Him. I will protect Him, for He acknowledges my name, He will call upon me and I will answer Him.* Call on God and listen for His answer. If you ask, God will give you the words that you need to say to be His ambassador and to avoid being wounded. Take a tip from teenagers. They're good at (not) listening to anger. Roll your eyes, and look up while anger is being vented. Let the angry words fall to the ground. Resist believing them.

Later then when the situation is calmer, follow what **Isaiah 1:18** says, *Come now, let us reason together, ...Though your sins are like scarlet, they shall be white as snow.* Reason together and forgive using the same love which overcame sin and death. Love wins over fear, anger and woundedness. Forgiveness and Love have to be the motivation used to solve problems. If the reasoning together doesn't work - prayer for reconciliation does work. See **Galatians 5:13**...*serve one another in love.* God's got all the answers. He is only waiting for you to ask Him for them, and make good use of them. Try smiling ! Do not speak a word of defense! Do not attempt to justify yourself in any way. Stand with your legs in a firm stance, lean back a little, and fold your arms across your chest. It says to the one who **Lost it**, "I know you're angry and I know you don't really mean what you are saying. We'll talk about this later, because right now I'm not listening! If I spoke, you wouldn't listen either!" Body language works. Besides it might make them laugh and break the whole conflict apart.

Where there is love, everyone wins. There are no losers to gloat over. Love is not a competition! Love doesn't keep score. Does your way of problem-solving work? If not, try God's way. Reason together, forgive and pray *after* the anger has subsided.

THE BLAME GAME

This game of condemnation is one of the most *unity-destroying*, time-consuming pastimes on the planet. Why is it that someone must <u>always</u> be to blame? The division between the blame-ERS and the blame-EES becomes a chasm too wide for any one to cross. Avoid acting out of pride and offense. We have a culture that is consumed with pointing the finger and spending useless time figuring out who was at fault rather than working together to resolve the problem. By the time someone is identified as the guilty one, the problem has intensified. Walls have been built by giving and receiving offense. **We tend to attack each other instead of the problem. Isaiah 58:9** says ...*if you do away with the yoke of oppression, with the <u>pointing finger</u> and <u>malicious talk</u>... then your light will rise in the darkness, and your night will become as noonday. The Lord will guide you always.* You have a choice: God's way or your way. Let your light shine. Love never shuts the door on relationships.

God's Word is just as true for our country as it is for family and all other relationships. Whose fault is it anyway, the Democrats or the Republicans? Divisive fault-finding and criticism are ingrained in our way of life. It seems that we as a nation and as families are more focused upon finding fault and criticizing, than in working together for the common good. Somebody always has to **lose**! No one wants to be a "loser". Swallow the pride of competition and forgive errors, either intentional or unintentional, and quickly move on to positive action. Take the problem to Jesus. Confess, repent, receive forgiveness, and BE DONE! Remember, God has promised to guide you *always*.

Hebrews 12:14 says *Make every effort to live in peace with all men and to be holy.* If you move from the darkness of condemnation and accusation into light and work together focusing a clear light on the problem, you will be in obedience to God's Word and receive His guidance. When you do your part of **Isaiah 58:9**, God will do His part. Examine <u>Heart-Attitudes for Self-Condemnation</u>, expressed either by outward actions or inner thoughts.

- I'll never forgive myself for __?__(any action, lack of action or spoken words)
- I don't know what I did, but I guess I'd better apologize anyway.
- What did I do to make you so angry?
- How can I make it up to you?
- I'm doing everything I know to do to stop the argument. What else do you want me to do?
- It's all your fault, if you hadn't done what you did, I wouldn't be so angry.
- It's your fault; you forgot to tell me what's going on. You got me into this mess.
- What? Didn't you listen to me? I know I told you.
- Can't you get anything right the first time?
- I failed as a parent, a friend, a spouse. I can't forgive myself for letting him down.
- I just can't be good enough to satisfy others.
- I know that it is my fault. I'll do better next time.
- This tragedy would not have happened if I had done what I should have done.
- I should have seen this problem coming, but I didn't.

CHANGE FROM SELF-CONDEMNATION
TO LEAVING JUDGMENT TO GOD

When you want to condemn your Self or others, seek God in prayer. Ask for His wisdom in the situation. Renew your mind by knowing in your heart that you are God's creation and that you were created in His image which is *good* <u>not</u> *guilty.* Jesus does not condemn us. He said in **John 3:17-18** *For God did not send His Son into the world to condemn the world, but to save the world through Him.*

For whoever believes in Him is not condemned... That is absolutely clear! How else can it be interpreted other than as it stands? To condemn your Self is to deny the truth of God's Word.

Be free of guilt and condemnation. You are a child of God, redeemed by the blood of the Lamb. Declare right now that you believe God's Word and that you will no longer bow your head in guilt, shame or self-condemnation before anyone. Follow Jesus' example.

2. CONNECT WITH THE HOLY SPIRIT IN PRAYER.

Father, God, I know that Jesus paid the price for my sin on the cross, but I don't know how to live without guilt and condemning my Self. When something goes wrong, I take responsibility for it and condemn my Self for not doing more to fix it. Help me to see that this is a conceit, a deception thinking that I alone am responsible for what happened. I cannot possibly be the only one responsible for negative events. To think that I am is to believe an absolute, ridiculous lie!! I ask forgiveness for assuming such far-reaching authority over everyone and everything. When I feel guilty, I am giving my Self all the credit for wide-spread negative influence in the lives of others. I repent of this false mind-set.

I repent of being quick to apologize for things I didn't do or for not doing more to avoid an uncomfortable, hurtful situation. I will come and confess my guilt to You every time I want to condemn my Self by assuming guilt that is not mine. I thank You, Lord, that through Jesus I can walk away cleansed from any sins. By receiving Your grace, I can now live forgiven and free of this Self-imposed burden of guilt and condemnation. God, I'm praying Your Word back to You. **Hebrews 8:12** *and* **Jeremiah 31:34** *both say that You... will forgive their wickedness and will remember their sins no more. Holy Spirit in me, help me to recognize when I'm remembering something that God has forgotten. Show me how to monitor my conversation and thoughts. I want to eliminate the word "sorry" when when I use it as an attempt to accept guilt for any action or circumstance that I did not cause.*

Please, God, give me wisdom to accept responsibility, to accept and to repent for my own sins--only, leaving the rest of this guilty garbage to rot.

I no longer want to be burdened and hindered in serving You. I will no longer receive all criticism as deserved, but I give it to You. I give up my over-sensitive conscience and false sense of responsibility to You. I praise Your name that I am now free of guilt AMEN (firm and established)

3. BREAK THE ROCK OF SELF-CONDEMNATION WITH THE HAMMER OF GOD'S WORD.

Mark your part and God's part, then meditate on those scriptures that speak to you personally. Select at least one verse of scripture to commit to memory and speak it out loud *when you are tempted to condemn your Self.* Choose as many verses as you need to break the influence of Self-condemnation in your life. Belief in God's spoken word will erase past condemnations

Before you meditate on these scriptures, you have to examine your belief that <u>God is greater than a deceptive, over-sensitive conscience</u>. By over-sensitive conscience I mean: believing that whatever is going wrong is in some way your fault. You didn't do enough. You should have seen it coming. You didn't work hard enough. There was something you should have done to prevent the problem, but you were neglectful and not paying attention. These are all lies and conceits, not to mention a waste of time by dwelling on what has already happened, playing the blame game with your Self. STOP IT! You will always lose. You are not the only one in the world who makes mistakes! Pray to God for the solution and wisdom for positive action.

Believe that the knowledge of God's Word is the knowledge of God, Himself. It is He who has declared His everlasting love. He knows the secret places of your heart even those you hide from your Self. In spite of your short-comings, your mistakes, and your doubts, God's love has *never* left you. **Psalm 103:13:** *As a father has compassion upon his children, so the Lord has compassion on His children who fear Him; for He knows how we were formed, He remembers that we are dust.* His love for you extends even beyond your brief life span to your children for generations to come. God's love and blessings are on those who love Him for a thousand generations.

SELECT MEMORY VERSES FOR MEDITATION

I have starred recommended memory verses.   Read all verses out loud.

1 John 3: 18-20 *Dear children, let us not love with words or tongue but with actions and in truth. This then is how we know we belong to the Truth and how we set our hearts at rest in His presence whenever our hearts condemn us.   For God is greater than our hearts, and He knows everything.*

Jeremiah 31:34 *God said, "For I will forgive their wickedness and will remember their sins no more."*

1 John 1:9 & 10 *If we confess our sins, He is faithful and just and will forgive our sins and purify us from all unrighteousness.   If we claim we have not sinned, we make Him out to be a liar and His Word has no place in our lives.*

Psalm 103:12 *As far as the east is from the west, so far has He removed our transgressions from us.*

Romans 8:1 & 2 *Therefore, there is now no condemnation for those who are in Christ Jesus, because through Christ Jesus the law of the Spirit of life set me free from the law of sin and death.* Declare out loud, "I am free!"

***John 8:11 *Then neither do I condemn you," Jesus declared, "Go now and leave your life of sin."* **Read John 8:1-24**

***1 Corinthians 4:3,4 Paul said, *I do not even judge myself. My conscience is clear…It is the Lord who judges me.* You can see that Paul did not judge himself, so do not judge *your* Self. God looks at your heart and will judge you with mercy, grace, and His perfect justice.

***Read. **Jeremiah Chapter 31** in its entirety for it is a message of great love and hope containing many encouraging words such as **verse 13** *I will turn their mourning into gladness. I will give them comfort and joy instead of sorrow.*

DECLARATION: I refuse to take criticism and judgment from others to heart and I will not respond with guilt to accusations or manipulations.   I serve God, not those who criticize and want me to do more to serve their own interests.

I am thankful to God that only He judges truly and rightly. I cannot be falsely accused. God will vindicate me. He will show me innocent.

I declare that God sees my heart while others see only outward appearances through their own agendas. I will not presume to rightly judge my Self, but let God be my judge. All other judgments I will not hold in my heart to weigh me down with Self-condemnation. I rely on the fact that Paul did not judge nor condemn himself when he had been guilty of persecuting the new Christians. He stood and watched as his order was carried out in the stoning of Stephen. But when Jesus appeared to him on the road to Damascus, he repented and was forgiven. I accept the same offer of God's forgiveness of my sins from Psalm 103. They are as far apart from me as the east is from the west.

I will walk according to God's will for me, freely relying upon His Word. Holy Spirit, I give You permission to stop every thought that takes criticism and turns it inward to Self-condemnation. I declare that I am free to be judged only by God, my heavenly Father. When I am tempted to condemn my Self, I will destroy that temptation with the hammer of God's Word which I have committed to memory.

THE ROCK OF
SELF-JUSTIFICATION

1. IDENTIFY THE ROCK OF SELF-JUSTIFICATION: *to prove to be right; to clear yourself from blame; vindication; sufficient grounds or reasons; sufficient grounds or reasons for forgiveness.*

The justification of Self is an effort on your part to soothe guilt and to excuse behavior for which your conscience or the Holy Spirit convicts you. You are not the judge! God judges you. You cannot judge your Self rightly for God's Word tells you that your heart is deceitful. You learn this Self-justifying behavior from the time that you are a small child. Do you remember pleading with parents, "But he started it, "and "He hit me first!"? You tried to be held less accountable or guilty than another by shifting blame. You also learned to look at the letter of the parents' rules in order to squirm out of punishment with words such as: "But you said…" knowing full what was meant by the rule but also knowing that the meaning did not match the rule's <u>exact</u> wording. Kids learn early to look for *loop holes* because they know how *legalism* works. They have learned to manipulate parents by appealing to their sense of fairness in order to get out of work or trouble. By the time they themselves are adults, they are past-masters of Self-justification.

Titus 3:1 *Remind the people to be subject to rulers and authorities, to be obedient, to be ready to do whatever is good.* These are the things that you should be teaching your children as well as consistency of ethics. You have to show them their spiritual boundaries outlined by God in His Word rather than let them hold you hostage with the accusation that you are being unfair because of a double standard or because, "Everyone else is doing it, so why won't you let me?" Teach God's boundaries before they get to school and stick to these boundaries yourself. Children are quick to see a double standard. When they do--- out the window goes any credibility of your parental discipline. If it's okay for you to do, they will do it too no matter what you say. Children need the security of boundaries. If there is no security, then there are no limits and rebellion becomes the *norm*. Rebelling against God is disobedience and willful deceit exhibited through justification of Self. It becomes a mind game that leads to lack of respect for authority, youthful rebellion against wisdom, and a life of strife.

Even adults fool themselves (other words for Self-justification) when they measure the degree of wrong with a slide rule called situational ethics. Sometimes things are right and sometimes the same things are wrong depending upon the surrounding circumstances. You may do something shady or indulge, just this once, in some questionable activity because no one is watching. As a Christian you are called to act with integrity in all circumstances. You represent Jesus to a world of unbelievers. How can others believe what you say but do not practice? If Christian ethics summed up in the two commandments of Jesus in **Matthew 22:38** don't work for you, then why would those same commandments work for unbelievers?

Spiritually, you as an adult may attempt to justify your Self because you are not as guilty as someone else. It's not unusual to hear people say something like, "I'm a good person" when they really mean, "I'm not a murderer or an adulterer". I go to church on Sunday". The Pharisees followed the letter of the law but not the spirit of the law. You forget that all are guilty of sin.

Justification of Self comes in many forms: "I'm right in doing what I did because everybody does it and nobody caught *them*," or "I have a legal permit which allows me to park here," when you are *not* the owner of the handicap tag. You are to obey the laws of the land – letter *and* spirit. You are representatives of Jesus. People who are watching you will judge your God by your actions.   I believe **"Hypocrite"** is the word unbelievers use to justify their own beliefs for continuing to move away from God. Watch your witness!

Romans 3:22-24 says, *This righteousness from God comes through faith in Jesus Christ to all who believe. There is no difference, for al! have fallen short of the glory of God and are justified freely by his grace through the redemption that came by Christ Jesus.* Self-justification is powerless. It does not work.   God is the only one who can justify. God has justified us and He defines the requirements for justification. God will not be mocked. You can't fool Him for He looks at your heart. You have no right or authority to even attempt to justify your Self to God. You may try to *deceive* yourself by justifying your actions, but Self-justification does not work with God.

Search for evidence of Self-Justification in Attitudes of your Heart, expressed either inwardly in thoughts or outwardly through your actions.

- I was right in doing what I did.
- I mean no harm. God wants me to be happy so it's okay to do this.
- I say things to convince my Self that what I did was okay.
- When I look at my Self in the mirror in the morning, I know that I'm a good person.
- I can prove to you that I was right.
- It's important to me to be right and that other people know that I am right.
- I haven't done anything wrong as far as I know.
- I feel that I need to explain everything so that people will know I have told the truth.
- I need to tell my side of the story. Then you will see who is right.
- I am not perfect. Nobody's perfect.
- I'm not as bad as _____ (person's name with whom you compare yourself and what he has done that is far worse than what you have done.) Put yourself in a good light.

- There's no law against what I did. I didn't hurt anybody else, only my Self.
- Why aren't you punishing that person? He did the same thing that I did.
- I don't deserve to be punished.
- If you have money you can get away with anything.

Before you go on to the prayer, MEDITATE on the Parable of the Pharisee and the Tax Collector found in **Luke 18:9-14.** The Pharisee *justified* himself to God. Now you know why Jesus said, "WOE unto you, Scribes and Pharisees" nine times in scripture. You cannot justify your Self to God. Substitute your name in the parable and see if this scripture shows you something about your Self: *The Pharisee prayed about himself: 'God I thank you that I am not like other men – robbers, evildoers, adulterers – or even like this tax collector'.*

2. CONNECT WITH THE HOLY SPIRIT IN PRAYER. PRAY:

Father, teach me to pray according to Your will. I ask forgiveness for any prideful, Self justifying prayers that I have prayed. I repent of attempting to justify my Self and my actions to You and to others. You see my heart and know what's in it. I ask for Your forgiveness. Help me to renew my mind so that I am alert to catch my Self in the act of justification and stop it. Holy Spirit in me, I give You permission to alert me when I speak or act to justify my Self in any way.

I no longer need to be RIGHT or pass on blame to someone else. There is no longer any point to doing that. Your standards are just for You are a just God. All I need to do is admit guilt, when I am to blame, then to repent of the act, and ask Jesus for forgiveness. I will then, be careful not to repeat what I just repented of. When I receive Jesus' forgiveness, then it is truly over and done with. I thank You, God that at that point, You forget my sin. Your Word says that You remember my sin no more. Now that I know this, already I can sense that I don't have to explain or justify my words, thoughts or actions to anyone. If I choose to give reasons for my behavior or beliefs, it will be out of a sense of caring, not out of justifying my Self or satisfying the demands of others so they will not think bad things of me. My explanations are not necessary because, God, You know the truth in my heart. Others will believe what they choose to believe. If I have been falsely accused, You will justify and defend me with Your truth. You will uphold me, validate me, and acquit me even when others won't. I desire to please You, my Lord and my God. AMEN (firm and established)

3. BREAK THE ROCK OF SELF-JUSTIFICATION WITH THE HAMMER OF GOD'S WORD.

Read these scriptures out loud more than once and meditate on them, particularly the two which are starred. Think how they fit into your life.

Because Self-Justification is a new concept to most people, the number of scriptures is lengthy. Select a few scriptures that you understand the best and memorize at least one of them so that when you are tempted to justify your Self, your chosen scripture may be spoken to resist the temptation.

Luke 16:14, 15 Jesus said to the Pharisees, *You are the ones who justify yourselves in the eyes of men, but God knows your hearts. What is highly valued among men is detestable in God's sight.*

Luke 10:29 *But he wanted to justify himself, so he asked…* In this scripture, an expert in the law was testing Jesus with a question so that he could be right and declare Jesus to be wrong. **Read Luke 10:25-37**. The expert was not Self justified as he had planned but instead was humbled by Jesus' answer.

Psalm 24:5 *He will receive blessing from the Lord and vindication from God his Savior.* Only God can vindicate you, clear your name, or defend you and lead you to victory.

***Titus 3:7 *So that being justified by His grace, we might become heirs having the hope of eternal life.* God justifies you through Jesus. God's grace justifies you. You have no need to do it. When you justify yourself you are in error, and in effect, prevent God from vindicating you.

Galatians 3:24 *So the law was put in charge to lead us to Christ that we might be justified by faith.* The letter of the law can become a way to circumvent real, spiritual obedience, allowing us to do things which the spirit of the law prohibits.

Acts 13:39 *Through him (Jesus) everyone who believes is justified from everything he could not be justified from by the law of Moses.* The law of Moses was not abolished. If you break one commandment, scripture tells you, you have broken them all. Jesus showed you a better way through forgiveness and grace. He paid for your sin on the cross. All you have to do is to turn away from your disobedience to God's Word. Ask for forgiveness, and you will be forgiven by a loving Father who, because of Jesus' sacrifice, sees your sin no more.

***Romans 8:33 *Who will bring any charge against those whom God has chosen? It is God who justifies.*

Psalm 119:116 *Sustain me according to Your promise and I will live.*

Psalm 41:12 *In my integrity you uphold me and set me in your presence forever.*

Psalm 62:6 *My salvation and my honor depend on God.*

Isaiah 41:10,11 *So do not fear for I am with you; do not be dismayed, for I am your God, I will strengthen you and help you; and will uphold you with My righteous right hand.*

Isaiah 42: 2 *Here is my servant whom I uphold, my chosen one in whom I delight; I will put my Spirit on him and he will bring justice to the nations.* Uphold is another way of saying justify. God will uphold you when you are falsely accused.

DECLARE out loud: **I am justified by my faith in Jesus. I no longer need to justify my Self to anyone for any reason because I walk in God's will. I do not seek to be right and prove others wrong in order to** *save face,* **maintain my Self respect, or achieve the respect of men. My only concern is to be justified in God's sight.**

I declare that with the Hammer of God's mighty Word, I have broken the Rock of Self-justification which I, my Self, have placed between God and me. Now nothing related to Self can stop me from receiving God's answers to my prayers. They are released, and in faith I receive them.

THE ROCK OF
SELF-INDULGENCE

You're not entirely to blame for all the pleasure-seeking that you do; it's all over America, like flags on the 4th of July. Advertisers and television commercials place temptations to indulge squarely in your face like candy placed at the grocery check out counter where children can't miss it. Americans can financially afford to indulge in treats of all sorts. Even those who can't, do so on credit cards. Indulgence is fun - but not consequence-free. It leads you away from God, not towards Him.

You really don't have to indulge your Self. God does it for you. Do you know that God is the most indulgent Father of all? He gave His people, the Israelites, everything that they needed. They didn't have to work for it. He gave them peace by driving out their enemies. He gave them the land for which they did not toil. He gave them houses they did not build. He gave them fruit trees and vineyards they did not plant. He gave them cities to live in. Read **Joshua 34:13**.

He gave King David the desires of his heart because David loved God and was obedient to Him. But, when David acted outside of God's will by taking another man's wife and causing the death of her husband, he was subject to the consequence of God's justice. God asked David why he had done these things when He reminded David He would have given him *anything* that he asked for within His perfect will. Anything not in God's perfect will has consequences. Perfect will is just that – perfect with no consequences.

PERFECT and WILL are key words. Worldly indulgence has consequences because the motivation for this indulgence is imperfect and outside of God's will. The ways of the world are not God's ways and tempt you to move out from under the protection of His love. They also entice you to act contrary to your own best interests. **Proverbs 16:25** says, *There is a way that seems right to a man but in the end it leads to death.* God knows what leads to life and He knows what leads to death. You do not have that wisdom, unless of course, you ask God for it. How many of us are going to ask God if it's okay to act on a Self-indulgent, pleasure-motivated urge? Not many! God would say, "No". David didn't ask if he could take Bathsheba as his wife because he knew in his heart it was against God's will. Of course God would have had to tell him, "No". Why do people fool themselves into thinking that they can fool God?

Your motivation for worldly indulgence in pleasure is altogether imperfect, deceptive, and short-sighted.   It leads to *grave* consequences, literally. You wouldn't allow a dangerous hunger to grow if you knew the price you would have to pay. That price is being out of God's plan for your life. It is a pre-meditated act of cutting your Self adrift from truth, beauty, peace, joy and all that God is--- to follow a physical or emotional urge.

God's motivation for His indulgence in you produces joy, peace, love, whatever you need in over-flowing abundance beyond your ability to comprehend and... without consequence. God adds no sorrow to His blessings.

God **cannot** do evil (harm you) by giving you something that you have no way of knowing will lead to your destruction.   If you *knowingly* choose the destructive direction, God will let you. He will not violate your freedom to choose. He knows your heart. Self indulgent prayers do not get "yes" answers. If you choose to indulge your Self, you're on your own!   When you move out from under the protective umbrella of God's will, natural consequences are unavoidable. God is not punishing you. You, in fact, do harm to your Self.

God promises you the desires of your heart. Why, then, are you settling for a chocolate fudge sundae, a new car, or other trivial temporary things that you quickly tire of, when you could have eternal joys beginning *now* on this Earth-- joys that are ever too great for you to understand yet? It's your choice. You can enjoy the results of over-indulgence in Godly pleasures now *and* later without limits because you are living according to God's will and His perfect plan for your life.

1. IDENTIFY THE ROCK OF SELF-INDULGENCE:

• *Pleasure-seeking to satisfy Self; self-gratification, sensualism, excess; undue gratification of one's appetites, desires, or whims; recognizing no limits or restrictions; ignoring warnings against over-indulgence; listening to only what you want to hear to justify over-indulgence.*

Identify <u>Heart Attitudes of Self-Indulgence</u>, either internally or externally expressed. The heart attitude of indulgence that I'm talking about here is not an occasional treat, but a way of life, a habit, indulgence without consideration for others or — most importantly — without <u>limits</u>. Indulgence is the ultimate focus on Self. No one else is in the picture — just you, your Self, and the pleasure of your indulgence. Could indulgence be considered another definition for Self-worship?

- I'm worth it. I deserve it.
- I owe it to myself.
- I love to pig-out on my favorite food.
- I'm going to regret spending all this money, but right now I'm having fun.
- I'm stuffed, but I can't resist more chocolate.
- I'll hate myself in the morning, but I'm going to have one more drink, one more helping one more...
- My credit card company loves me: I fill it up and sometimes max it out.
- I shouldn't have looked at the new hi tech stuff because I know I can't resist upgrading.
- I'm feeling depressed, but I know just what will bring me out of it — a shopping spree – a new fancy putter - a new trick for my truck - CHOCOLATE!

- Gotta' have the latest gadget, the best putter ever, biggest truck, that vacation I can't really afford.

Some indulgences are innocent enough, but there are those which are harmful to your body. Other indulgences (another name for pleasures) are harmful to your budget, your finances, and many times your relationships. Often indulging in favorite things can result in bodily injury, but when reasonable limits are exceeded, indulgence borders on Self-destruction.

The fruit of Self-indulgence is most often an aftermath of *dis*-satisfaction mixed with a lot of *dis*-comfort and guilt. Example: My 2 year old daughter discovered that butter was **good** so she took a fresh quarter pound stick of butter from the table into the back yard, sat down in the grass and ate the whole thing. She knew that she was being "sneaky". There was no one in sight either to guide her **or** to stop her. There was no warning about eating too much of a good thing (limits) and what happens (natural consequences) when you do. Eating the butter was messy fun while it lasted, but then the consequences set in - a greasy kid results in bath time and a tummy- ache, which in turn results in yucky pink medicine. If you want the world's pleasures which you can see, more than you want God's love and provision which you receive by faith, you'll find a way to be sneaky rather than obedient.

Often adults say, "Never again! I learned my lesson!", but they repeat that behavior of over-indulging at holiday time, birthdays, and after a big meal (another word for over-indulgence) which results in nap time and often uncomfortable indigestion. We conveniently forget that we will have to face the physical consequences of that extra piece of pie. There is no lasting positive result or spiritual fruit in the indulgence of Self, only momentary satisfaction. Think ahead! Don't loosen your hold on common sense. Be Self-controlled. **1 Corinthians 6:19-20:** *Do you not know that your body is a temple of the Holy Spirit whom you have received from God? You are not your own. You were bought at a price. Therefore honor God with your body.* Knowing this scripture puts over-indulgence in perspective. Remember!

You are not your own.

One of the fruits of the Spirit is Self control, the opposite of Self indulgence. Indulgence by its very definition reaches the point of excess, where it loses any beneficial qualities that moderate amounts of gratification might produce. Examples of common over-indulgence are: anger, sleep, self-pity, a hobby, snacking, watching television for hours at a time. Almost anything can be done to the point of excess perhaps even to the point of addiction. You need the Holy Spirit to help you with Self control, for God sent His Spirit at the request of Jesus to dwell within you and teach you. You have to desire Self-control and deliberately practice temperance in all things, because a mature Christian exhibits the spiritual fruit of Self-control.

Self-control is the only truly positive **Self** word. It places Godly controls on all others. You are recognized by your fruit. **Galatians 5:22:** *So I say, live by the Spirit and you will not gratify the desires of the sinful nature.* Your sinful nature (a desire to Self-indulge or over-indulge) is in conflict with the Holy Spirit. Read **Galatians 5:16-26** for a list of the fruits of the spirit and **Matthew 7: 15-20** for more details on identifying people by their fruit.

1 Corinthians 9:25 explains, *Now every athlete who goes into training conducts himself temperately and restricts himself in all things. They do it to win a wreath, that will soon wither, but we do it to win a crown of eternal blessedness that cannot wither.*

You don't have to give up all your favorite things – just do not over-indulge or use them as a crutch when you are emotionally challenged. God is your Strength and your Refuge, your Hope and very present Help in time of trouble--chocolate is not. Perhaps you would be more willing to seek God's face in times of trial and temptation if He were made of chocolate or maybe even--coffee? Choose to change from Self indulgent to God indulgent.

YOUR FIVE SPIRITUAL SENSES

Change from the limited satisfaction of your natural senses to the satisfaction of your spiritual senses. All of the five natural senses have spiritual counter-parts, and are also spiritually gratified in the Bible. Go ahead, over-indulge in God's Word. This hunger satisfied by indulgence, will change your life. When was the last time you fed your spirit? Do you hunger and thirst after righteousness? You probably do, but don't recognize it. It's sort of like you want something, but you don't know what it is. It's like an itch that you don't know where to scratch. It's like a yearning, but you don't know what for. So you go to the refrigerator and stand there looking for something that might satisfy this spiritual hunger with the same food you would use in satisfying your natural hunger. That uneasiness, discontent, restlessness may be God calling you. When you don't recognize His call, you may answer such a spiritual call by doing something like eating or drinking something, which does not satisfy but adds pounds and inches. Remember you have spiritual senses and a **hunger for God** is one of them. Feast on God's Word. Such a hunger cannot be satisfied with natural things but will give peace to your body, soul, and spirit. Check out what you hunger for!

Self-indulgence leads you away from God with all the natural consequences and discomforts, but you cannot over-indulge in God. You can have as much of Him as you want. There are no limits. **1 Peter 1:14:** *As obedient children, do not conform to the evil desires you had when you lived in ignorance.* Explore your spiritual senses.

TASTE: There are so many scriptures that "fill you" until you want no more. You will be supremely satisfied so that you no longer desire to over-satisfy your flesh. You will have found something infinitely delicious and pleasurable to your spiritual sense of taste.

Psalm 34:8   *Taste and see that the Lord is good.*
Psalm 119:103   *How sweet are Thy words unto my taste.* All you can eat is available to you calorie free.

Galatians 5:16-17-- *So I say, live by the Spirit and you will not gratify the desires of the sinful nature. For the sinful nature desires what is contrary to the Spirit. Your spirit and sinful nature are in conflict. You cannot satisfy the one with the other.*

SMELL: God gave you senses that pleasure your body, but He also gave you senses to pleasure your spirit. These spiritual senses are powerful. Explore the spiritual sense of smell. Take, for example, God's sense of smell: *The Lord smelled the pleasant aroma...* The account of why God decided not to flood the earth again (or could be so literally interpreted) is partially because of God's pleasure in His sense of smelling Noah's worship. Read it and decide for yourself - figurative or literal? **Genesis 8: 18-22.** God gave *exact* directions in the Old Testament as to the contents of the fragrant incense that was to be burned upon the altar of the Tabernacle. Incense symbolized the prayers of the people, and God took pleasure in the burning of that sweet incense. Why would God add pleasure to man's sense of smell, unless it was first a pleasure to Him? Is the sense of smell a practical necessity only? Think about it.

TOUCH: Discover your spiritual sense of touch. The healing touch - **Mark 5:3, Luke 22:51, Matthew 9:29**; the Life-giving, resurrection touch - **2Kings 13:21**; the Angelic touch - **1 King 19:5.** Explore this sense on your own. It will lead you closer to God.

SIGHT: Check out your spiritual sense of sight. There is beauty in the holiness of God. How does one see God's holy beauty except spiritually? People in the Bible saw the messenger angels of God that spoke to them. Visions and dreams are spiritual "sightings" which can be more vivid and real than this world we see. Can you imagine what it was like to be John and spiritually see what he wrote in the **Book of Revelation?** Read **Isaiah Chapter 22.** Read **Habakkuk Chapter 2.**

Read **Joel 2:28** and **Acts 2:17** to learn that God will pour His Spirit on all people, and they will all have visions and dream spiritual dreams. God-dreams are so different from your natural ones. Usually you do not see them with your natural eyes.

SOUND: Your spiritual sense of hearing emanates *from* your spirit, not your natural ears. It is a knowing, an intuition-like sensing. You sort of hear Jesus' voice "in your head" but it is not your imagination. Jesus said in **John 10:27**, *My sheep listen to my voice; I know them, and they follow me.* Read **John 10:1-18** and **John 11:25-30**. Some things can only be discerned spiritually and hearing the voice of God or hearing Jesus calling you is an important one. For times when people actually heard God's voice with their ears, read about Samuel who heard God calling him with his natural ears in **1 Samuel Chapter 3.** Read about Paul on the road to Damascus who literally heard the voice of Jesus with his natural ears in **Acts 22:6.**

Once you stop focusing on what your natural senses tell you and believe that you are a spirit being that has a soul and lives in a body, everything begins to make sense regarding how you connect to God with spiritual senses. If you are not born again in the Spirit and/or don't believe that you have spiritual senses, then how can God communicate with you Spirit–to-spirit? Think about it.

Your flesh is not the sum total of your being; that's why the body can never be completely satisfied by Self-indulgence. The satisfaction you are looking for is found spiritually by being God-indulgent. Indulgence can also work in reverse where you indulge God giving Him all the glory, praise, adoration, worship, and obedience. He enjoys watching you prosper in His Word. Why does He care so much about you anyway? You've known the answer ever since you became a Christian. He gave His only Son to reconcile – redeem you - back to Him, so that He could have fellowship with you. He loves you and returned love is always welcomed. God **is** **love** and you are to love Him with all your heart, soul, strength, and mind. Go ahead! **Over-indulge God!** God's Word for over-indulgence is "delight". You are to delight yourselves in Him, and He delights in you. Sounds like a spiritual shindig to me!

2. CONNECT WITH THE HOLY SPIRIT IN PRAYER.

Communicate with God Spirit-to-spirit. Try out your spiritual senses. Ask the Holy Spirit to help you focus on God with those senses. Hearing probably will be the easiest to begin with. You have to **expect** to hear. Jesus said you know His voice. Listen during prayer when meditating on His Word, or just sit quietly - wait and focus on Him. Sing or hum your love to Him. Scripture tells you to *Sing and Cling* to God expressing your love to Him.

PRAY: *Holy Father, You know my weaknesses, even those of which I am not aware. I want to change my focus from using my natural senses to discover and develop my spiritual senses. Holy Spirit, teach me how to do this. Lord, You have said in* **Proverbs 15:8** *that You delight in the prayers of the upright. I want to give You pleasure through my prayers. I want to delight in Your blessing by receiving, enjoying, and thanking You for each one. It is my delight to be Your child and as my Father, I know that You delight in me. I need not seek to be satisfied by the pleasures of the world, for they satisfy but a moment while Your Holy Spirit satisfies my spirit for eternity. Only You can delight my soul filling me with Your perfect love. I can still enjoy the world that You created, but true, complete, satisfaction comes not from satisfying my body with indulgences, but from being in Your presence. Mold me, Lord; make me according to Your will. You satisfy my longing soul and my mouth with good things.* **(Psalms 103:5 & 107:9)** *I desire Your tender love and provision which satisfy my soul and spirit completely.*

My Self-indulgent habits often lead to over-indulgence and are hard to break. I ask You now to help me to change from seeking to satisfy my Self to seeking to please You. Lord, I hunger and thirst for Your presence. I allow You free reign in my life to show me how to make this awesome change, and I thank You that I have Your Holy Spirit to guide me. I can do all things through the power of Jesus who strengthens me. You have given me everything that I need to do Your will in my life. I delight in Your voice and Your touch. Show me how to also delight in Your visions and dreams, in tasting Your Word, and how to experience the sweet fragrance of Your presence. Blessed are You, my Father, Who knows how to give good gifts to me, Your child. AMEN (firm and established).

3. BREAK THE ROCK OF SELF-INDULGENCE WITH THE HAMMER OF GOD'S WORD.

Do not forget to locate your part and ⟨circle⟩ it in each scripture, then locate and <u>underline</u> God's promise. Select at least one scripture to memorize. Write it on your heart and use it when you are tempted to indulge your Self. Temptations will come in many forms. Just remember that the symptoms of spiritual hunger are: restlessness, uneasiness, don't know what to do or what you want to eat, sometimes depression, not knowing what you want. Not being able to sleep may be a call to prayer. Try satisfying these desires with prayer. You may be surprised that God has been calling you to prayer and you have not known it.

1 John 2:16-17 *For everything in the world – the lustful cravings of sinful man, the lust of his eyes and the boasting of what he has and does – comes not from the Father, but from the world. The world and its desires pass away, but the man who does the will of God lives forever.*

In **Titus 3:5,** Paul says: *At one time we, too, were foolish, disobedient, deceived, and enslaved by all kinds of passion and pleasures... But when the kindness and love of God our Savior appeared, He saved us, not because of righteous things we had done, but because of His mercy. He saved us through the washing of rebirth and renewal by* the Holy Spirit.

***James 4:2, 3 …*you do not have, because you do not ask God. When you ask, you do not receive because you ask with wrong motives, that you may spend what you get on your pleasures.* Could this be a reason for your unanswered prayer?

2 Timothy 2:22 *Flee the evil desires of youth and pursue righteousness, faith, love, and peace, along with those who call on the Lord out of a pure heart.* These scriptures may seem to say to a worldly-focused mind that you must give up all pleasure. Not so! But rather to give up *seeking* the pleasures of the world to seek and receive the greater joys and pleasures of God. This is an exchange. It's a good deal – a real bargain! You give up the fleeting temporary – yes - even the harmful pleasures that destroy the body and soul , to receive the joyful pleasures of the eternal. But--only if you do your part. If all you believe in are the now-pleasures of this world that you can see and experience, you will not seek God for His Holy Spirit. The understanding of eternal things written in His Word will remain a mystery. Feed your spirit on the truth of God's eternal Word. Enjoy His presence.

James 4:7-8 Submit *yourselves then to God. Resist the devil and he will flee from you. Come near to God and He will come near to you.* (What's your part? What's God's part?) Worldly pleasures and indulgences are deceptive, offering much, but when continued, they destroy. Happiness depends upon circumstances and the pleasure of the moment. You give that up for the "Joy of the Lord". God's eternal love supplies for all your needs – physical emotional, spiritual. The same previously mentioned conditions apply when you want to come to God: 1) Love God, 2) Acknowledge God, and 3) Call to Him. The pleasures which tear down your body and entice you away from God are called sin. It kills the body, the soul, and the spirit. **Proverbs 14:12&13** *There is a way that seems right to a man, but in the end it leads to death.*

It's possible to have a weird idea of sin. God does not want you to indulge in anything that hurts you He just happens to call

all the attractive, worldly stuff that hurts you — sin. Part of the problem is that you may look at the moment rather than beyond it. The big thing about sin is that you don't know the danger of it. It looks good to you, or it feels good at the moment so you don't know why you aren't allowed to have it or enjoy doing it. God knows what you don't know or understand! He protects you from your ignorance. He protected Adam and Eve in the garden by telling them *not* to eat of the Tree of Knowledge of Good and Evil. God made a list of what He finds detestable, that is, harmful to body, soul, and spirit. See **Deuteronomy 18:10**. What's harmful is all in your perspective. God's not taking stuff away from you; he's protecting you like any good parent, to keep you from hurting yourself with attractive temptations. He gives you good gifts. In **Matthew 7:11** Jesus said, *If you, then, though you are evil, know how to give good gifts to your children, how much more will your Father in heaven give good gifts to those who ask Him.*

Most of us avoid or don't like the word sin. It's scary and rather unsettling to say the least. You may think that you are required to give up all the good things to follow Jesus, It looks like you don't get anything from God that is that much fun in return. Would you willingly give up something that tastes good because you know drinking it causes disease or destroys your body? Would you willingly give up something that looks inviting and beautiful, but is toxic? Would you willingly give up anything that causes pain and suffering to you or to others even though it seems temptingly inviting? Could you give up your favorite vice which you enjoy to receive something infinitely better that you cannot see? You have to *believe* that what God offers is immeasurably better when experienced with your spiritual senses than with your natural senses. You have to **know** that your body is not your real self: You *are* spirit. Your body was nothing but an empty, fleshy "thing" before God breathed His Spirit into it.

Develop your spiritual senses so that you can know what good things you are receiving when you give up desiring the deceptive, temporary worldly pleasures classified as **sin**. It's a "no-brainer" from there! From God you get: **Joy** – unspeakable, **Peace** - that passes all understanding, **Love** - that's unconditional, **Power** -strong enough to overcome all obstacles. When you are born again you are a new person in Christ Jesus. Your mind is renewed and you have *five new spiritual senses.*

Remember your part and God's part of scripture?. You get good gifts promised by God (that's God's part of the scripture) if you ask Him and fulfill His requirements (that's your part). Of course, you still have to examine your motives when you ask. If you are asking for pleasure that will harm you, cause problems to you in your future, or cause harm to someone else, you won't get what you ask for. That prayer might seemingly go unanswered. The answer is "No!" God will not give you a stone when you ask for bread. You have to trust God that He knows what will be harmful to you, just as your children have to trust that you to keep them from harm. If they want something that they shouldn't have, they may pitch a fit if you don't give it to them. They may even hold their breath until they turn blue. Giving them the harmful things they want is unthinkable! They don't know about the worldly dangers to their bodies and souls. You do, so you protect them.

You don't know about **spiritual** dangers, but God does. He protects you from the spiritual dangers, the sin that you are not able to see. God is **not** keeping you from the "good stuff", He's just has a picture of the future that you can't see. If you could see what God sees, you wouldn't choose the destructive pleasures of over-indulgence in comparison to the wonders and unspeakable joy that God has for you. Now that you understand the reality of spiritual senses , you can ask to **see** what gifts God has for you and your loved ones.

*****Ephesians 4:22 -24** *You were taught, with regard to your former way of life, to put off your old self, which is corrupted by its deceitful desires; to be made new in attitude of your minds; and to put on the new self, created to be like God in true righteousness and holiness.* This is a good scripture to commit to memory. Read all of **Ephesians Chapter 4 and Chapter 5:1-21.** Make it a goal to put off your old Self and put on the new godly Self. **STOP RIGHT**

NOW AND THNK OF HOW YOU CAN DO THIS. If nothing comes to mind, pray for God to show you how.

For more details see **Galatians 5:13,** *You, my brothers were called to be free. But do not use your freedom to* <u>indulge</u> *in the sinful nature.* You still have the choice to rebel against God. Read also **Galatians 5:16&17;** see **Galatians 5:19** for a list of what sinful nature is. Read all verses 19-26. Read also **Galatians 6: 1-10 and Romans 13:14.**

DECLARE: I will no longer serve two masters—my Self which advocates indulgence and my God. My Self has to go because is in constant conflict with God's purposes. I choose to follow Jesus, my Savior. He did nothing but what he saw the Father do. I will delight in the law of the Lord and be obedient to Him. I desire to delight in God and look for Him to delight in me. I receive God's peace that passes all understanding. I will be obedient to His Word. I declare that I will no longer indulge my Self in harmful worldly pleasures and pursuits. I will listen to God's voice, exercise and develop my spiritual senses so that I may experience spiritual pleasures. From now on I put on my *new Self* created to be in God's likeness. I am in agreement with God's plan for my life. With joy I desire to serve my Lord and my God only.

THE ROCK OF
SELF-SEEKING

1. IDENTIFY THE ROCK OF SELF-SEEKING: *Careerist* • *seeking fame or fortune; may be evidenced by excess of gambling, scheming, calculating, fortune hunting, self-loving, acquiring to gain, opportunistic/opportunist*, one who waits for events before declaring his opinions or shaped his conduct to circumstances of the moment in order to take whatever advantage is to be had. <u>Personality type</u>: grasping, wheeler-dealer, get-rich-quick; looking for an edge over someone else; acquiring to gain by one's own efforts. Lays up or collects; accumulates hoards, amasses things of value to excess.

<u>Examine Heart Attitudes for Self seeking</u>, expressed either by outward actions or inner thoughts.

- You have a hunger and thirst for position of authority over others, either social or financial, as a way to get what you want.
- You would wear a T-shirt saying, *Momma Loves me Best* and be serious about it.
- You want your share of the action.
- Me First! Attitude.
- What about me? I just want to get what's mine.
- You are very aware of status; wanting the newest and the best of everything, whether you can afford it or not. Hoping that your fortunes (luck) will change and that then you will be able to pay for your life-style.
- All you want is all there is and then some. More is better.
- I believe that the one with all the toys wins, and I want all the toys.
- I make unrealistic comparisons to others who appear to

have more than I.

- That's not fair! I deserve the credit. I deserve more recognition or salary than that person. He must be a relative of the boss.
- I think I deserve advancement rather than the one who was promoted. I've been here longer.

Read the parable of the workers in the vineyard. **MATTHEW 20:1-16.** Jesus said in **Matthew 20: 16,** *So the last will be first, and the first will be last.*

CHANGE FROM SELF SEEKING TO GOD SEEKING

When you seek to benefit your Self, there will never be enough to satisfy you. You will always want more because you see those who have more. When you begin to seek God, not for Selfish gratification but for love of Him, He will supply all your needs and an additional overflowing measure as well.

God says in **Malachi 3:10:** *"Bring the whole tithe into the storehouse, that there may be food in my house. Test me in this," says the Lord Almighty, "and see if I will not throw open the floodgates of heaven and pour out so much blessing that you will not have room enough for it.'* Choose to trust in God's promise of abundance for your finances instead of scheming and calculating on how to get your own fortune.

2. CONNECT WITH THE HOLY SPIRIT IN PRAYER.

PRAY: *Lord, God, I confess that I have made my job an idol by giving it all my time and devotion. There is little time for my family, for prayer, and for meditation on Your Word. My job has been an all-consuming focus in my quest for recognition and financial security. I turn to You, my God, for wisdom and help to bring back a godly balance in my life.*

I pour out my heart to You. I want to trust You at all times for all my needs. Lead me in Your path of righteousness and truth. I forsake my desire to follow my Self-chosen path looking for temporary wealth. recognition, and security to follow Your loving counsel through the Holy Spirit in me. Now, rather than seek opportunities to get wealth and get ahead, I will seek opportunities to do Your will and to spend time with You. I belong to Your eternal kingdom so seeking for things in this world no longer makes sense. You will supply my needs. You will advance me in position as I am ready, willing and obedient to Your Word.

Thanks for not giving up on me when I would not see the error of desiring Self-fulfillment above all else. Your mercy endures forever. I receive Your love and choose to build a new God-seeking, not Self-seeking focus in my life. AMEN (firm and established)

3. BREAK THE ROCK OF SELF-SEEKING WITH THE HAMMER OF GOD'S WORD.

Select at least one scripture to memorize and use against any Self-seeking that tries to return and block your prayer answers. I recommend starred scriptures.

James 3:16 *For where you have envy and selfish ambition, you will find disorder and every evil practice.*

***Matthew 6:33** *But seek first the kingdom and His righteousness and all these things will be given to you as well.* I did this and it changed my life!

Mark 9:35 *Sitting down, Jesus called the twelve and said, "If anyone wants to be first, he must be the very last and the servant of all."*

***Galatians 6:4** *Each one should test his own actions, then he can take pride in himself without comparing himself to somebody else.* You cannot follow someone else's road to success. You must follow the one that God has prepared for only you. Ask God to reveal His will for your life.

***2 Chronicles 15:2** *The Lord is with you when you are with Him. If you seek Him, He will be found by you, but if you forsake Him, He* *will forsake you.* Get <u>with</u> God.

Lamentations 3:25 *The Lord is good to those whose hope is in Him, to the one who seeks Him.*

If you are not walking with God according to His will, you're on your own! Whatever happens rests squarely on your own shoulders as your responsibility. That's the difference between doing things *your* way or doing them *God's* way. God does not fail, and when you trust in Him, <u>He will not let you fail.</u>

To understand the fruit of seeking worldly success, read the parable of The Rich Man and Lazarus, as told by Jesus in **Luke 16:19-31.** The rich man succeeded in achieving everything he ever wanted, but he missed it! He got only what the world had to offer. He did not know that <u>God had a *better offer*</u> which was much, much more than he could ever dream. He could have had it all if he had believed and acted on God's word. He was satisfied with the world's promises and had no need to seek God. In **Proverbs 8:21** God said He is ... *bestowing wealth on those who love me and making their treasuries full.* See also **Luke 18: 18-25, Matthew 6:19-20, 2 Corinthians 10:12, Psalm 103:2-3.**

DECLARE out loud: I am a seeker of God and His righteousness; I forsake Self-seeking and desire to re-focus my life on the teachings of Jesus. I will now seek to be involved spiritually and emotionally in my family showing and giving the love and attention that was once consumed by my job. God will show me where to find the time to balance work and family. My God will help me through the Holy Spirit Whom He has sent to dwell within me.

I expect the things of God to bear fruit in my life, not the empty temporary material things of this world. I will search for God with all my heart and all my soul, and He will provide for me as He promised. I know that His Word is true. He will add to me all that I need in abundance. To God be the glory.

THE ROCK OF
SELF-SATISFACTION

1. IDENTIFY THE ROCK OF SELF-SATISFACTION: • *Complacent, puffed up, self-approving, self-congratulatory, self-righteous, and smug. Got it made; cocksure; self-opinionated; superior; confident in the flesh; glad that you are not like others.*

Identify <u>Heart Attitudes</u> of Self satisfaction. Look for evidence of Self-satisfaction inwardly hidden or expressed in your past actions.

- I don't mind telling you that I did a great job.
- No one else could have done better than I.
- I'm satisfied with what I did – better than the average and then some.
- Now I can rest a while after a job well done.
- I'd like to see someone do it better.
- I did great, didn't I?
- I've done all there is to be done.
- No one can top this.
- I can't hear too many compliments. I like to hear them. I deserve them for my hard work.
- I got it made. I can sit back and relax now, coast a little, and enjoy my success.
- I enjoy getting the glory, being recognized publicly for the hard work I've done.
- I am pleased with the knowledge that I appear good in the eyes of others.
- I like being in control and taking the credit.
- When others are recognized for their good work, I have feelings of jealousy. I want what they are receiving. My work is just as good or better. I should have been recognized publicly.

Sometimes your many selfish pursuits result in short-sighted, unforeseen consequences. You can only see in hindsight how you could have succeeded if you had worked with others towards a common goal. Too late, you often realize that the Self-satisfaction of personal accomplishment ends up hollow, empty of the satisfaction that you anticipated. You may wonder, "Is that all there is?"

Consider **Proverbs 14:12:** *There is a way that seems right to a man, but in the end it leads to death.* Physical and/or spiritual death is indicated by the context. When focused on your own satisfaction, that way which seems so right, may possibly lead unintentionally to the death of relationships, marriages, and dreams. You have no way of knowing the end result of your pursuit when you begin it. If you leave God out of your plans, your way may take you where you do not want to go. God's plan for your life will bring you your heart's desires. God sees the dangers, snares, and pitfalls which you cannot see, and He directs you around them no matter what it looks like to you. He even warns or stops you from continuing on your way into dangerous territory. If you do not accept the Lord's advice, **Proverbs 1:31** says, *They will eat the fruit of their ways and be filled with the fruit of their schemes.* Think about it and learn wisdom. If the source of your Self-satisfaction is wealth and riches, then what have you sacrificed to get them? Are the sacrifices worth it? Consider the following scriptures.

Ecclesiastes 5:10 *Whoever loves money never has money enough; whoever loves wealth is never satisfied with his income.*

Proverbs 19:23 *The fear of the Lord leads to life: Then one rests content untouched by trouble.* Resting content means: delight, fulfilled, pleased, untroubled, peaceful and happy. God alone satisfies us.

READ **Matthew 6:25-34** for the enumeration of your needs. Consider and meditate on Matthew **6:33:** *But seek first the kingdom and His righteousness and all these things will be given to you as well.*

DECLARE: I exchange Self-satisfaction for God-satisfaction and I receive His promise of contentment and peace. I will ignore attempts of others to tempt me to a higher-paying or higher-

status job unless God tells me that's where He wants me. I will be alert to the signs of dis-satisfaction and realize that I need to seek God's wisdom for direction. I thank God that His satisfaction enriches my life.

2.

CONNECT WITH THE HOLY SPIRIT. Use these words for meditation and prayer.

O, Lord, my God, I ask You for forgiveness for any selfish decisions I have made to create my own satisfaction. I have determined anew to follow Jesus and this time endure and continue without being double-minded by part time serving my own choices and secondarily giving lip-service to following Jesus. I set my heart on things above and not on worldly pursuits. I confess that I have at times sought them and found little satisfaction in whatever success I have achieved. You are my treasure, God, and Jesus is my Lord. I give up my Self satisfaction, and I desire to be fruitful so that others may see Jesus in me. I want to be the good tree of Your Word that bears fruit - the fruits of Your Holy Spirit: peace, love, joy, gentleness, kindness. And above all I desire the one fruit most difficult for me -- Self- control. For I am as Paul when he says in Romans 7:19, "I have the desire to do what is good, but I cannot carry it out. For what I do, I do not want to do; the evil I do not want to do---this I keep on doing."

Lord, I confess to You that I have often thought of Self-satisfaction as a natural outcome of Self image building, well-deserved pride of accomplishment. That is a conceit and a deception. Without those who worked with me I could have done nothing. Instead of leaning back and being satisfied, I now desire to recognize others whose work was well done. You have put me together in community with others. I can do nothing, have nothing, accomplish nothing without the body of Christ and those who have gone before me and prayed for me. I desire to serve others in Love. To claim accomplishment for my Self is not according to Your Word.

I ask Your forgiveness and Your wisdom on how to focus on Your will for my life. You deserve the glory. When people see me, I now want them to see Jesus in me. My goal will be to show others an example of how Jesus would have us live together in Love and share the sense of accomplishment. Teach me, Holy Spirit, to share acclaim with others and to give You the glory. I have sought satisfaction based upon my own Self-focus and false beliefs, instead of seeking Your truth. For my ways are not Your ways,

111

*O God. Your Word says in **Isaiah 55: 8-9,** For my thoughts are not your thoughts, neither are your ways my ways, declares the Lord. As the heavens are higher than the earth, so are my thoughts than your thoughts.* Lord, write these words on my heart.

*Your ways, O Lord, are too high above my ways to understand. Show me how to exchange my unbelief for a strong faith in Your Word. You invite me with **Psalm 34:8,** Taste and see that the Lord is good. Lord, please show me how to taste Your goodness spiritually.*

*Lord, only when I seek You for who You are and through a relationship with Your Son Jesus, can I find peace and be satisfied. I long for that joy, unspeakable and spiritual satisfaction that cannot be achieved from worldly success. The hope of the world tantalizes me with rainbow after rainbow and another hill beyond the next hill. With the meeting of each personal goal, there arises another one beyond it where I believe satisfaction awaits. You called me to come to You on Your holy mountain-- to come into Your presence where I long to be. Too long have I wandered aimlessly in the wilderness of worldly pursuits seeking for fleeting moments of satisfaction. I know now, that the satisfaction of my heart's desires can be found only in Your presence. Lord, I place You on the throne of my heart to direct my ways. I cannot control my thoughts without You. I desire to bring every thought captive to Jesus **(2 Corinthians 10:5).** I will follow You, Jesus to where You have always been – in the presence of the mighty ever-loving Father. Savior, like a shepherd lead me, much I need Your tender care. AMEN* (firm and established)

3. BREAK THE ROCK OF SELF-SATISFACTION WITH THE HAMMER OF GOD'S WORD .

Don't forget your job and God's job - underline and circle. Record in your scripture notebook any outstanding verses which meet your specific needs.

Psalm 103:5 *Who satisfies your desires with good things so that your youth is renewed like the eagles.* God satisfies you.

Luke 12:18 The Parable of the Rich Fool. *Then he said, 'This is what I'll do, I will tear down my barns and build bigger ones, and there I will store all my grain and my goods. And I'll say to myself 'You have plenty of good things laid up for many years. Take life easy; eat, drink and be merry.'*

112

Psalm 91:15 *With long life will I satisfy Him and show Him my salvation.* This promise is for those who truly love and trust Him.

Ecclesiastes 3:13 *That everyone may eat and drink and find satisfaction in all his toil-- this is the gift of God.* Declare that you receive this gift in your life, now.

Additional scriptures: **Psalm 90:14 and Isaiah 58:10, 11**. Read **Isaiah 55**. God's wisdom will amaze you.

DECLARE: I have sought satisfaction in my own pursuits - more money, more time to do what I want, more attention and understanding from those that love me. Every satisfaction that I achieve turns out to be only another step towards seeking more satisfaction. I am eating food without substance. It leaves me hungry, always wanting more. I declare that only the Love of God can fully satisfy me, and only the Holy Spirit can completely fill me. I choose to seek Him – first! Self satisfaction no longer stands between me and God. I declare the Rock of Self-satisfaction destroyed by the hammer of God's Word.

THE ROCK OF SELF-PITY

1. IDENTIFY THE ROCK OF SELF-PITY: *Feelings for one's own sufferings and misfortunes; self-misery; tending to act in such a way as to make people feel sorry for you to gain sympathy and attention in order to feel better; "The Charlie Brown Syndrome".*

Self-pity is just a few tears away from Self-indulgence. We laugh at the children's song, "Nobody likes me, and everybody hates me. I'm going to go and eat worms." Wallowing in the misery of Self-pity is no laughing matter, but a way of life for some people. They have list upon list of all the bad things that happened to them from the time that they were born! Both Christians and unbelievers have lists. They have never forgotten or dealt with one thing on their list. Instead of doing something to change things or seeking God, they re-enforce their woe by repeating it to anyone who will listen.

I have been stopped in stores by strangers who tell me tales of woe. I listen, give them a quick prayer that they did not ask for, and go on leaving them to God. They just want someone to listen. That's okay. However, when they stop someone else in the next aisle, I notice that they repeat the same story over again. It's obvious that listening doesn't help. People have to overcome the Self Pity Trap into which they have fallen. Neither be a "feeder" to self-pity nor a "receiver" of self-pity. It sneaks up on you touching your emotions before you can recognize the trap. You may find yourself feeding the same problem you are trying to eliminate.

Everybody has days when things go wrong, but by the attitude of your heart, you either determine to overcome those times or to allow them to dominate your life. Choosing to seek sympathy through re-experiencing these problems, repeating them over and over to any one who will listen perpetuates and intensifies the problems. Worst of all, it creates a victim mentality. This is not God's will for His children. He has made us victors – not victims.

STAMP OUT SELF PITY BEFORE IT MULTIPLIES

You are a compassionate listener and representative of God's unfailing love. When presented with a long list of misfortunes of a friend *re-direct* their thinking away from glorifying the negative, towards glorifying God. Help the "pity *full*" person to see what God had done and is doing in his life. If he is not Christian and resents your *preaching* to him, speak encouraging scriptures, re-worded so that he does not know that you are speaking directly from the Bible. Set the power of God to work in his life. Steer him away from that arm-long list which further embeds the problems. God will show you how to discern the Litany List of woes of those who desire nothing but sympathy from those who want a solution and are ready to accept positive input.

Never-no, *never* sit passively and listen to a pity-filled person whose sole purpose is to suck your spirit dry. There is no glory to God in that. They have no intention of changing or doing anything about their situation. Leave them with a word of promise from God as seed if they are willing to receive it, but do not linger through **false compassion** or guilt. Be sensitive to the leadings of the Holy Spirit.

EXAMINE your Heart Attitude. Look for any of your own residual Self-pity. Pity, or lack thereof, manifests in your behavior and your innermost thoughts. The following suggestions are intended to trigger past or present attitudes so that you can deal with them in prayer.

PERSONAL SELF-PITY
- What about me? What am I—chopped Liver?
- Why does everything go wrong for me?
- Why doesn't anybody call me? Doesn't anybody care?

- Am I a bad person?
- RATS! I knew that would happen again!
- What's wrong with me? What can I do to make people like me?
- I often need to ask people for help. I'm not sure that I can do things alone so I don't try. I have had too many problems when I do things. It seems that I never succeed. Someone can do it better for me.
- Why don't I have many friends?
- Why does everything bad always happen to me?
- When am I going to get a break?
- I never get chosen for the high profile stuff. I get left-overs that nobody wants.
- I'm always last. People treat me as if I'm a loser so I don't expect to succeed.
- I would sing the Old Hee-Haw song about gloom, despair, agony, and bad luck if I could just remember the words.
- I make people feel sorry for me by my actions and things I say.
- My name is *Ineeda*. I need -a- this and I need -a- that!

SELF PITY PERSONALITY TRAITS

Self-pity is used to manipulate. It draws others into a sphere of influence by using their unsuspecting love, compassion, and desire to help to feed a starving soul . Tears almost always work. Deliberate manipulation by facial or vocal expression work too. Needy or high-maintenance people want all the love and sympathy they can get, but there is never enough. They are like the outer space "black holes" that suck everything into the depths of darkness.

MIS-PLACED PITY FOR OTHERS BOUND IN **SELF**-PITY

There are those who are willing to receive compassion, but not willing to give any. See the parable of the Wicked Unmerciful Servant in **Matthew 18:32.** Those who pity themselves fail to see similar situations experienced by others. They refuse to help another in genuine need because of a personal superior attitude. They judge others who are actually more deserving of compassion as: pathetic, shabby, wretched, hopeless, and helpless. They often reveal these attitudes in statements such as: "I lived through it; so will you. You knew the hurricanes would come again; why did you rebuild your house in the same place? Why should I help you when you don't make any effort to help your Self? Live with your mistakes. You will know better next time. Get a life!" Consider **Proverbs 19:1**. *He who is kind to the poor lends to the Lord, and He will reward Him for what he has done.* God's Word is the standard for genuine caring for the unfortunate. Discernment gained from a quick prayer to God will show you the difference between fake and genuine need.

PUBLIC PITY

Another facet of this lack of genuine compassion for the misfortunes of others is rooted in doing good in order to be seen, loved, and rewarded for the good deeds that others see you do. This attitude also is based on another form of being "needy" to draw people into your sphere of influence. Read all of **Matthew 6:1-4. Verse 3** states, *But when you give to the needy, do not let your left hand know what your right hand is doing, so that your giving may be in secret.*

Romans 12:15 *...weep with those who weep.* Allowing God's love to manifest through you, results in being *...a living sacrifice, holy and pleasing to God. This is your spiritual act of worship.*

STRATEGIES FOR OUTSMARTING THE SELF PITY SPIRIT

Be alert in dealing with those who exhibit Self pity. Avoid being sucked into the position of agreeing with them, thereby strengthening their need for more pity. Refuse, in a loving and kind way, to do things *for* them thereby not becoming their guilt-driven servant. Offer them practical help by working *with* them and offer spiritual help by praying *with* them. Do things *with* them – not *for* them. Do not allow Self pity to be in control of the relationship; you as God's ambassador are there to offer a way out of the "pity-pit". Point them to God. If they aren't receptive, at least you planted a seed.

Self pity is a trap, a snare to draw unsuspecting, caring people into co-dependency thinking that they are doing good. When this happens, the needy person draws people into an *ungodly* sphere of influence. They make *you* their god and provider. You can't *really* help them, but God can. You can lead the Self pity-er away from desiring help and attention from people, by showing them how to come up out of the self-perpetuating pity lifestyle into a relationship with God. If they refuse to receive a warm-hearted concern for their spiritual well-being, then be encouraged that you have planted the seeds of God's Word and know that you did not help them along on their downward Self-destructive path. If you do nothing but sympathize and co-operate with them, you are playing the "Spider and the Fly Game", sort of like the spider tempting the fly into its web from which there is no escape, only death. The spider of Self Pity feeds on the unsuspecting sympathizer. The more pity it gets, the stronger it becomes. Self Pity is strong, but God's compassion is stronger and smarter. He cannot be deceived. When in doubt, check with God in prayer.

SPIRITUAL REMEDIES FOR YOUR OWN TEMPTATION TO PITY SELF

Sing God's Praises. Go to God for comfort in times of trouble. Read and sing God's words of faith instead of falling into the Self-indulgence of food, entertainment, and addictive behaviors. If you have noticed, the Psalms are meant to be sung and David, I'm sure, did sing them with harp accompaniment. You'll notice that the Psalm begins with praise and a recounting of that entire list of what God had done for him instead of a list of woes. He expresses his faith and then urges others to seek God. His focus is entirely on God and not on his problems. At the end he declares absolute assurance that God is in control. David's song lifted him above his dire circumstances. You can do the same. Sing the psalms of David. They will do for you what they did for David. Keep your focus on God.

Psalm 34:1 & 18 can dispel your gloom and cloud of despair. David sang this Psalm in a time of distress. He had a just cause to pity himself, but instead he rose up from the darkness he was experiencing to focus on the light of God's provision.

Verse 1 *I will bless the Lord at all times; his praise will always be on my lips.*

Verse 18 *The Lord is close to the brokenhearted and saves those who are crushed in spirit.*

READ WORDS OF COMFORT FROM GOD

Read God's Words aloud for your Self or someone else so that your spirit can hear them. Remember that you have spiritual hearing and your spirit is strengthened and fed by God's words. Your faith increases as you listen to the Word of God. Read **Psalm 27:14, Psalm 37:39, Psalm 46:1-3, 2 Corinthians 1:5, Matthew 11:28, Nahum 1:7.** These scriptures are your weapons against the temptation to pity your Self.

If there is no Bible available where you visit a pity person, bring an easy to read version with you and read aloud from it, saying something like: "These words helped me when times were hard." Even if they just listen politely, God's Word will still be activated in their lives by your faith. Remember you are not the one doing the ministering; the Holy Spirit, the sword of God's Word, is doing the job. The pressure is not on you to do anything. You are God's loving messenger, His ambassador. Pity cannot stand against faith and love.

Psssst!!!! Forget to take your Bible with you when you leave.

2. CONNECT WITH THE HOLY SPIRIT IN PRAYER.

PRAY: *Thank You, my God, for meeting all my needs - spiritual, physical, and emotional. When I need comfort, You are there. There is nowhere that I can go where You will not find me. When I need cheer, You are there. When I need soothing and rest, You are there calling me to come to You, for You are there waiting to give me peace.   You have promised to draw near to me when I will draw near to You. When I need contentment, You are there to enfold me in Your loving arms filling me gently with Your peace.*

There is no need to feel sorry for my Self in times of trouble or distress. No one except You can always be "there" for me. You never sleep! You know my needs even when I haven't yet realized that I have a need. You have promised never to leave me. I am weak and only You know the fullness of my weaknesses. Jesus said that Your strength is made perfect in my weakness. **(1 Corinthians 12:9)** *I thank You that it's okay for me to be weak because You are my strength. Whenever I need support and there is no one available to encourage me, I will read Your Word out loud **and encourage my Self** in You.*

Lord, I receive Your loving-kindness.   Teach me to show Your tenderness to those in need. I ask for a loving, discerning tender heart that sees where pity is needed and where firmness and speaking the Truth of Your Word will reveal deception and manipulation. AMEN (firm and established)

3. BREAK THE ROCK OF SELF-PITY WITH THE HAMMER OF GOD'S WORD

Remember to find your part and God's part then speak His Word out loud against the rock of Self-pity. Select at least one verse to memorize and recall when you are tempted to feel or act out of pity for your Self.

1 Peter 3:8 *Finally, all of you, live in harmony with one another, be sympathetic, love as brothers, be compassionate and humble.* If you follow this scripture you will be giving genuine compassion, neither giving nor receiving the Self-kind of pity .

Philippians 4:19 *My God will meet all your needs according to His glorious riches in Christ Jesus.* Do not rely on other people to meet your needs. Ask God for what you need. He WILL supply. Prayers of Self- pity will never be answered by God.

2 Corinthians 4: 8&9 *We are hard pressed on every side, but not crushed; perplexed, but not in despair; persecuted, but not abandoned; struck down, but not destroyed.* You will have hard times, but there is no need to pity your Self. Your God is faithful to keep you from destruction.

Romans 8:28 *We know that in all things God works for the good of those who love him, who have been called according to his purpose.* Look for the good, something to praise about, not trouble to complain about. God will get you out of the trouble not because you complain and grumble against Him, but because He loves you.

Ephesians 4:32 & 5:1 *Be kind and compassionate to one another, just as in Christ, God forgave you. Be imitators of God, therefore as dearly loved children, and live a life of love just as Christ loved us…* Be forgiving of your Self and others. If in your actions, you model after Jesus, you will never fall into the pity trap. You will have an abundance of love to share.

DECLARE **I declare that God has mercy on me. Therefore, I do not need to pity my Self. He is my Comfort and Shield, my Help in times of trouble. I will not allow my natural emotions to lead me into pity , either Self pity or misplaced pity where there is evidence of deception. When tenderheartedness seems to be required, I will ask God for wisdom and eyes open to see His truth. I will be able to separate those in genuine need from users and abusers.**

I will resist the temptation to feel sorry for my Self by immediately declaring that God supplies for all my needs. I will seek His face in prayer to claim His promises of rest, restoration, love, and provision. The word *pity* **no longer applies to me, but to others whose needs I can see as I am aided by God's wisdom. I will give generously of my time and my finances when God reveals a genuine need. Thank You, God, that Your great love is always there for me. All I need to do is call on Your name and** *believe.* **You will hear and call me close to You. TO GOD BE THE GLORY FOR THE THINGS HE HAS DONE IN ME.**

THE ROCK OF
SELF-CENTEREDNESS

1. IDENTIFY THE ROCK OF SELF-CENTEREDNESS: *narrow,*
● *self-serving, self-interested, selfish, egotistic, greedy, mean, inward
focus; refuse to budge or compromise; seldom want to change anything in
life; the way it is--is the way it must be.*

Identify <u>Heart Attitudes of Self-Centeredness</u>, whether inwardly
evident or outwardly expressed. Pray. Listen for the voice of the
Holy Spirit to show you any Self centered attitude. Repent of
each identified attitude as you progress through the following
list. Attitudes expressed here fit any age group from children to
the elderly. Not only are you looking to identify your own Self
centeredness, but the attitudes of loved ones to whom you may be
called to minister.

- I am the planet. You and all others are satellites in orbit
around me.
- This is my world and I let you in, but you must follow me,
give me what I want for I am **needy**. You must live by my
rules or I will reject you. There is no inner peace in this one-
person world. I stick with the things that I like and that I
think work for me. Don't try to change me. I will fight you
tooth and nail.
- If you want a relationship with me, it's on my terms only.
You give. I take.
- You must accommodate me and my schedule.
- If I don't get enough attention, I accuse you of not loving me
enough or caring for me.
- I have no desire to change. I have made my own world and I
think that I am happy in it.
- I am strict in requiring you to follow the rules of my one-
person universe.

- I am quick to let you know when you have failed to follow my rules or to please me.
- I always tell you I love you, but I do not express that love. I have no love to give away.
- I am too busy loving myself and maintaining my universe the way I like it.
- I have no patience. I am critical and inflexible.
- I will give money, but no time or of myself. Maybe I'm not willing to give at all. I offer criticism of the ministry of God or a particular expressed need in order to avoid giving. Needs of others do not intrude upon my one-person universe.
- Changes, especially unexpected ones, are disturbing and I complain to you about them.
- I will make everyone around me unhappy when I am unhappy.
- I am a high-maintenance person in need of attention, love, gifts, and comfort. I need constant reassurance. You can never give me enough of your time and your love, but you must keep trying to please me.
- I have a self-image of being a nice person. I don't understand why people avoid me.
- Few can tolerate or choose to tolerate my Self-centered behavior. Those who do, only increase the strength of my egocentric domination.

TWO KINDS OF SELF–LOVE

<u>Self centeredness is one kind of Self love, but God-centered love of Self is quite different</u>. There is no room for God in selfish love. When Self reaches the level of supreme focus of the soul, it becomes the object of worship; that is, it becomes an idol. By drawing all attention inward towards Self, it originates and controls desires -- emotional and physical -- and becomes the driving force of the will. As a result, all things circle about and submit to, the dominating influence of the insatiable Self.

Those who allow this kind of Self–ish love to reign on the throne of their hearts will often claim to know and serve God. With their words and actions they appear to love God in the religious fashion of the Pharisees, but their motivation is to control, to have the right answer, to draw others to Self and the system that supports it. God receives no glory. Those who are Self centered, are spiritually unable to bear good fruit and to prosper in body, mind and spirit.

In order to discover **the God-motivated, holy Self-love,** examine what God's word identifies as love and compare your innermost thoughts and motivations with what God says in **1 Corinthians Chapter 13.** This is the Love chapter, the truth of God, which is the measure of all things. Pray before you begin to spiritually discern and make comparisons. Pray that the Holy Spirit will guide you and that the light of God's amazing love will reveal to you any dark or hidden selfish love.

I have divided the love lists of **1 Corinthians 13:4-8** into four sections so that it will be easier to meditate and compare. These sections are: 1. What love is 2. What love does 3. What love is NOT 4. What love does NOT. I am using only the words from the NIV scripture except where I have placed brackets. Note that you will find different phraseology in other translations.

WHAT GOD SAYS LOVE IS

What love is:
> Love is patient. Love is kind. [Kind can mean: affectionate, compassionate, gentle, giving, good, gracious, hospitable, loving, tenderhearted, thoughtful, understanding.]

What love does:
> Always protects, always trusts, always hopes, always perseveres. Love rejoices in truth. Love never fails.

What love is not:
> Love is not proud. Love is not rude. Love is not easily angered. Love is not self-seeking.

What love does not:
> Love does not boast. Love does not envy. Love keeps no record of wrongs.

LOVE NEVER FAILS
[Fail can mean: abandon, cease, desert, die, disappoint, fade, forsake, give up, neglect, weaken]

This is the God kind of love, freely given to you so that you will be able to practice it and produce the fruit of His Spirit. You cannot have and give this kind of love from your own will and by your own strength. God is love. Unless you love God and have a personal relationship with Him, you cannot show the **1 Corinthians 13** kind of love.

LOVE NEEDS A RECEIVER
Before you compare your kind of Self love with God's intended " love of Self," know who is to be blessed in receiving this love. There has to be both a giver *and* a receiver. You have to have love in order to give it. You have to give it in order for it to be called love. Love is a giving, active word. You can't just *have* it. What you have is not love if you hold on to it. It is like the Dead Sea which receives fresh water from the Jordan River but has no outlet. Without a current to move it, circulate it, and keep it clean, it stagnates. It loses the characteristics of the fresh water.

Love must, by definition, be given. God gives us love so that we can be blessed both in the receiving as well as in the giving. Love originates with God. You cannot manufacture it.. It flows from God to you. You cannot pray for someone that you do not love. Consider your Love "Savings Account". How much love can you afford to give away through prayer? Do you know that everlasting, boundless love comes from God Who keeps your capacity to love full and over flowing?

Jesus gave us two commandments in **Matthew 22:37-39** Jesus replied, *Love the Lord your God with all your heart and with all your soul and with all your mind. This is the first and greatest commandment and the second is like it: Love your neighbor as yourself.* 1) You are to love God. 2) You are to love your Self. 3) You are to love your neighbor. You cannot love your neighbor until you first love yourself. But, before that, you must have the love of God to give. Then you can love your neighbor as you love your Self. The God-kind of love that you have for Self is the same measure of love Jesus tells you to give to your neighbor. If you're not sure who your neighbor is, before you continue, read the Parable of the Good Samaritan in **Luke 10:30-37.**

COMPARE

Now you are ready to make a comparison of your inner thoughts and feelings with how Jesus commanded you to love. You have three areas to consider. First, how do you love God? Second, how do you love your Self? Third, how do you love your neighbor? Return to the four divisions of God's idea of love in **1 Corinthians 13** as previously listed. Match your thoughts with God's Word.

GOD - Compare how you love God with how the scripture tells you to love Him. Meditate on the first commandment Jesus gave regarding your heart, your soul, and your mind. Look at each one. Don't be discouraged. Make a decision to love as you are commanded. God will help you. We all have a tough time measuring up to God's standards. Ask the Holy Spirit in you to increase your desire to Love God more, to love Him passionately, not just casually. Also ask Him to help you by showing you how to truly love Self and others. He will teach you, but you do have to ask expecting that He will. That's why Jesus asked God to send the Holy Spirit to you. You need spiritual, supernatural help. You cannot love like God does with your own effort. Love as Jesus commands.

YOUR SELF - Compare how you love your Self with how 1 Corinthians 13 tells you to love. Go through each of the four sections thoughtfully. Jesus infers that you must love your Self before you can love your neighbor. If you find that you don't measure up in that area, now that you know you need to love your Self, do something about it. Learn to always trust God. Learn to keep no record of your own wrongs. You have asked Jesus for forgiveness; you have been forgiven.

Do not be disappointed in your Self. Do not give up on your Self. Be thorough. Many of us are very hard on ourselves, then, consequently, we are just as hard or even harder on our neighbor. Be patient with your Self. Love your Self. If you see that you are not loving and patient with your Self because of false beliefs about your worthiness, you will not be able to obey Jesus' command to love your neighbor.

YOUR NEIGHBOR - Now, last of all, look at your love for your neighbor. You are to love your neighbor as your Self. If you have discovered that you do not love your Self as scripture indicates, but instead you have bought into worldly deceptions, go back to **1 Corinthians 13**.Repent of this false kind of love and be forgiven. Discover the areas that need a change-over when compared with scripture. Ask the Holy Spirit to help you love your Self the way God intended. You are a child of God. You have the love of God the Father in you. This is your inheritance as His child. Identify any <u>other kind of love</u> whether it is an intellectual, mind-centered love, something resembling love, having some characteristics similar to love, or an emotion suggestive of love. *Reject these kinds of love.* When you love your Self in an unconditional, God-like way rather than a Self-ish way, then you will be able to fulfill the second commandment of loving your neighbor *as yourself.*

SELF-CENTEREDNESS IS CONTROLLING, SELF-ISH LOVE

If you have self-ish love, it is Self-centered, Self-powered, Self-motivated, Self-gratified. It is defined as wholly regarding one's **Self.** Self-ish love has no sense of restriction, accountability or control. People who rebel against the Word of God by worshipping Self have deceived minds and seared consciences. They may claim to know God, but their consciences do not recognize Him, and consequently, they do not lead Self controlled lives. Read the three very short chapters of the **Book of Titus.** If Self is not under the control of your spirit, you are compelled to search inward for emotional, intellectual counsel. **The Self must be controlled and its limits spiritually defined.**

PAUL, TITUS, AND PETER URGE
CONTROL OF SELF

You are responsible for controlling your Self. Self-control cannot function without first making a decision to place limits on its desires and actions. Make a decision to stop every negative thought before it can grow. Once you make a decision to monitor your body's insistent urgings and desires, you will regain spiritual control of your life. Decide to keep strong, negative emotions in check so that they cannot get you into trouble with family relationships. Monitor your thoughts also. Stop negative thoughts at the outset so that they cannot generate problems or anger. These limits to Self will bring you peace *and* keep you out of trouble. Your spirit must be in control. Take steps now to strengthen your spirit with daily prayer and meditation on God's Word.

Follow Jesus. Remember the **23rd Psalm.** Deliberately walk where Jesus leads. He will lead you beside the still waters in peace and restoration. He will lead you in the path of righteousness to holiness. He will walk you through the valley of the shadow with his protection and comfort. God knows where He is going. His plan is far superior to any plan your Self may put together. Your Self has no clue to the truth of its destination or how to get there because it does not have the knowledge and wisdom of God. Paul, Peter, and Titus walked with God and understood the importance of controlling the Self. They needed Self-control and so do you. What they did, you can do.

PAUL   **1Thessalonians 5:6** *Let us be self-controlled putting on faith and love.* Make a choice to be Self-controlled. Remember that you have spiritual ears. Read God's Word out loud so that your spirit-man can hear, be strengthened, and remember what he has heard.

TITUS   **Titus 1:8** A mature Christian in leadership must be *...one who loves what is good, who is self-controlled, upright, holy and disciplined.* You need the inner strength of the Holy Spirit to control your Self-motivated desires and actions. If you are a leader in the church body, examine the integrity of your Self-control.

Titus 2:12 *For the grace of God that brings salvation has appeared to all men. It teaches us to say, "No" to ungodliness and worldly passions and to live self-controlled upright and Godly lives in this age...* If you desire to be in leadership in the body of Christ, be sure that you measure up to God's standards of Self control.

PETER   **2 Peter 1:5-8** *For this very reason, make every effort to add to your faith goodness, knowledge; and to knowledge, self-control; and to self-control, perseverance; and to perseverance, godliness; and to godliness, brotherly kindness; and to brotherly kindness, love.* Add these things to your faith in order to escape the temptations caused by your wordly desires. You need Peter's list for spiritual strength and prosperity.

1 Peter 5:8, 9 Be *self-controlled and alert... Stand firm in the faith.*

1Peter 4: 7 *Therefore be clear minded and self-controlled so that you can pray.* If you are not clear-minded *and* Self controlled, the implication is that you cannot pray as you ought. Since prayer is your connection with God through the Holy Spirit, you must control your Self. One of the fruits of the spirit which identifies you as a follower of Jesus is Self-control. You have to desire to be Self controlled and to remain on guard against slipping back into Self-*ish* control. It can happen before you realize it. Self-control is a life-long commitment and a key to getting answers to your prayers. Stay alert. Maintain your spiritual integrity.

The real issue is not as much love of Self as it is of Self-focus and spiritual boundaries. Self attempts through worldly temptations, to usurp God's position as the supplier of your needs both spiritual and natural. It wants all the glory and worship due to God. Its aim is to become the final authority in a believer's life totally destroying his relationship with God. But God made provision for just such a predictable situation. He provided an early warning system, a loving support system, and the eternal truth of His Holy Word written to guide all who seek Him. The Spirit of God teaches you, but that is not enough. You have to *choose* to learn. Pray David's **Psalm 27:11** and part of **Psalm 32:8,9** which are *paraphrased* into prayer form:

> *Lord, teach me Your ways. I want to do Your will. I thank You that You have promised to counsel me and to watch over me. If I act like a mule who refuses to do as his master wishes, I give You permission to alert me of my ignorant actions. I willingly choose to follow where You lead. I trust You and Your Holy Spirit within me. AMEN* (firm and established)

GOD'S BOUNDARIES TO RESTRAIN SELF-ISH CONTROL

Self rebels against God's boundaries. Therefore, God has applied limits in the form of a conscience. Self-*ish* love is then limited from within by the Holy Spirit and without through the Body of Christ around us. The focus of Self-*ish* love is on personal needs, desires and gratifications. Self recognizes no limits, no boundaries, and creates none of its own. The Self-*ish* love allows itself to do anything it chooses without reason or accountability, the restriction of right or wrong, or of ignorance of both natural or spiritual consequences. It does not look ahead to see the threatening destination of Self-destruction looming in the future. In short, all that is recognized by Self is the here and the now and the gratification of the moment. God says that whatever you sow you will also harvest — unless you are repentant and ask for His grace. This is both the law of nature and God's law. **1Thessalonians 5:6** says *Let us be self-controlled putting on faith and love.* Choose to control your Self and chose Life.

CONSCIENCE IS A BOUNDARY
God's Provision for Controlling Self-Centeredness

Conscience is defined as *the knowledge or consciousness of our own acts and feelings of right or wrong with a compulsion to do right.* Conscience is God-given and your first line of defense against the control of Self-centeredness.

Paul said in **Romans 9:1,** *I speak the truth in Christ – I am not lying, my conscience confirms it in the Holy Spirit.* Your conscience is accountable to and motivated by the Holy Spirit in you. It is a reliable boundary for the Spirit-filled Christian.

1 Timothy explains in **Chapter 4:2** that there will be those who abandon the faith, *hypocritical liars whose consciences have been seared as with a hot iron.* A conscience can be seared with a hot iron. Every time you ignore your conscience and over-ride it with Self-*ish* Self-will, you become less sensitive to its voice. When the hot iron (self-will or rebellion) renders our conscience insensitive to the Holy Spirit, He is unable to warn you when you cross the boundary from godliness to sin.

John 8:1-11 tells you that your conscience may be convicted by the Holy Spirit when confronted with the truth of God's Word. Jesus confronted the men who were ready to stone the woman caught in adultery. Jesus said, *If any one of you is without sin, let him be the first to throw the stone at her.* The men left one at a time. They did not stone her because Jesus confronted them with their own *personal* sin. Their consciences confirmed their guilt and compelled them to act rightly.

THE BODY OF CHRIST IS A BOUNDARY
God's Provision for Administering Boundaries to Self

You are the church, the Body of Christ. You and I are brothers and sisters in Christ Jesus. We live in love and peace together as one with Jesus as the Head of the Body of believers. As you, the Body, act in love according to the scriptures, you must act as **Titus** directs you in chapter **1: 13**, *Therefore rebuke them sharply so that they will be sound in faith...* Rebuke means to put to shame, reprove, check. The reason for rebuke is to speak to your brothers in love, not accusation, when they have been Self-deceived or have walked away from God. This is done in order that they may hear God's Word and return to His truth.

The body of Christ is to follow Jesus' example. He did not accuse nor condemn the men who would stone the woman caught in adultery. He merely allowed them to see through the eyes of their consciences that everyone, themselves included, has sinned. Likewise, Jesus did not condemn the woman or punish her. He allowed her to go free. Sometimes you need to be reminded that God did not send Jesus into the world to condemn, but to save. How could he at the same time both condemn and save? How could he then be the Son of a just God? It is far better for you to stand Self-accused and to humbly seek God's perfect will within the Body of Believers, than to continue in sin disregarding the limits of both your brothers and your conscience. God will stop you! He is not willing for any one of us to be lost. You have a choice to receive rebuke from the Body and return to God's will or to continue to rebel until God allows circumstances, or His agents to bring you to your knees. He does this in order for you to repent and turn back to Him. The bad fruit of your actions is *not* God punishing you, but rather the reaping of what you have sown. When you sin, you willingly walk out from under the provision of God's grace, His unmerited favor. God stands watching and waiting for you to return as did the father in the parable of the Prodigal Son. God is willing to throw Himself upon you in a loving embrace, forgive, and return you to a place of honor. What a celebration of God's forgiving love this is for us! Read **Luke 15:11-32.**

2 Timothy 3:16 *All scripture is God breathed and is useful for rebuking and correcting and training in righteousness so that the man of God may be thoroughly equipped for every good work.* God's Word is the instrument the body is to use in returning those who stray from the lighted path of God. Sometimes it is necessary for individuals in the body to ask forgiveness from the person in need of rebuke, before confronting in love, because they, themselves, have gossiped about or judged him . In **Luke 17:3,** Jesus said, *So watch yourselves. If your brother sins, rebuke him and if he repents forgive him.* Do the rebuking God's way – in love, motivated by love.

GOD'S WORD IS A BOUNDARY
God's Provision for Accountability

You are made accountable to God and to those whom God has chosen to lead you. You are responsible for all Self-ish, ungodly choices and actions, for God has commanded you to rebuke those in the Body who do not see the error of their ways. You are not exempt. If, however Self still rules despite the work of A. conscience directed by the Holy Spirit and the B. rebuke from the Body of Christ, even then God will not allow you to be lost! He will act as He has stated in His Word. C. He, Himself, will discipline you whether you have sinned deliberately or acted in ignorance.

Hebrews 12:5-7 *My son, do not make light of the Lord's discipline, and do not lose heart when He rebukes you, because the Lord disciplines those He loves and He punishes everyone He accepts as son. Endure hardship as discipline. God is treating you as sons. For what son is not disciplined by his father?* God will not allow you to continue unchecked on your path of Self-*ish* love. You are asked to endure punishment because you have refused to respond to the godly counsel of the Body of Christ and the warnings of your conscience. You still have a choice. If you choose to go the way of Self, God will not be idle. If you do not respond to God's discipline, His Word, His will, and the conscience instilled in you, He will allow you to reap what you sow. God will give you up to your unrepentant sinful ways. Israel is a prime example of what God will do when you turn away from Him towards Self in rebellion.

ISRAEL: AN EXAMPLE OF SELF CENTEREDNESS AND CONSEQUENCES

Israel's love for God grew cold. They worshipped idols. They turned their backs on God. Their hearts turned to stone. **Psalm 81:11,12:** *But my people would not listen to me; so I gave them over to their stubborn hearts to follow their own devices.* Even though the Israelites went through the motions of worshipping God, He saw the truth in their hearts. **Isaiah 29:13** *These people come near to me with their mouth and honor me with their lips, but their hearts are far from me. Their worship of me is made up only of rules taught by men.*

God also told Isaiah to tell His people, Israel, that for a time He would close their ears and their eyes and make their hearts calloused. Then there would come a time of destruction. See **Isaiah 6.** The people would then see what it is like to live as they had chosen--

without God's love and protection. But, no matter how long His people stayed unfaithful, He took them back when they cried out to Him. He restored them to His favor and they prospered as His people once again. God made a covenant with Abraham and Israel. He can never break that covenant. Even if Israel breaks the covenant, God will remain faithful. You have a share in the blessings of that covenant with God

God warns us in **Proverbs 14:12,** *There is a way that seems right to a man, but in the end it leads to death.* Better to return to God, humble yourself before him, and ask forgiveness than to insist upon continuing the way of Self that leads to death. God will not violate your free will. If you choose to continue in your wicked ways and walk away from God, His love will not let you go. Up until the very last milli-second of your life, God provides the opportunity for you to choose life. **Ezekiel 36: 26-37** tells what God will do when you return to Him and know that He is the Lord. *I will give you a new heart and put a new spirit in you; and give you a heart of flesh.* [Meaning a teachable, pliable heart] *I will remove from you your heart of stone. I will put My Spirit in you.* Read the remainder of **Chapter 36** for more details of what God will do when He restores you.

So you see, no matter how far away from God you are, or no matter how long you wander the trackless waste of Self, if you return to your God, He will bless you and forgive you. Learn a lesson from God's people. They went through many seasons of extreme and unnecessary misery when they followed their own Self-centered direction away from God. Sacrifice your Self-centeredness, your Self-focus , your Self-love and live in the Joy of the Lord. Now you have an understanding of how great is God's love as explained in detail in **1Corinthians 13:13 and 14:1** *And now these three remain: faith, hope, and love. But the greatest of these is love.* Follow the way of God's Love demonstrated to you through Jesus.

PRAY: *Lord, God of mercy and grace, I ask forgiveness for my past indulgence in Self-ish love. I desire to become Self-controlled. I know that I cannot do this alone for my body and soul see so many things of the world that are to be desired. They continually tempt me away from You. Strengthen my spirit making it stronger than both my body and my soul so that I can bring them into agreement with Your holy word. I make this decision to be strong in You, Lord, and mighty by Your power rather than continuing in the weakness of giving in to the deceptive desires of body and mind. I desire more of Jesus and less of me. I desire for Jesus to increase in my thoughts and actions, and that my Self will decrease in those Self-centered thoughts and actions. I know that I am asking these things in Your will because they are made clear to me by* **1 Corinthians 13 and Peter, Paul and Titus.** *I thank You for Your Holy Word that guides me. I will walk in it. 'Your word is a lamp to my feet and a light for my path.'* **Psalm 119:105.** Without the light of Your word, I would walk in darkness. I choose Your light! *AMEN* (firm and established)

DECLARE: **It is done, and I will not return to my former ways of being centered in Self. You are my God and I will praise You for the wonders and depths of Your mighty, faithful love for me. I am free to hear Your answers to my prayers.**

STRATEGIES FOR MINISTERING TO OTHERS TRAPPED IN SELF-CENTEREDNESS

When ministering to a spoiled child, a demanding elderly person, or anyone trapped in Self-centeredness, redirect their demands from you to God. You cannot help anyone by reinforcing unreasonable behavior. Such an attitude of co-dependency does more harm than good. When loved ones dominate you through guilt and Self-pity, they are in charge. A dramatic change is needed here! Until the proverbial mountain stops coming to Mohammad, and you the satellite, continue to abide by the rules of the master of the one-person universe, there will be no need for the universe to change.

You, your Self, are challenged to break out of the gravitational pull of the controller in such a way as to lead him/her into a new relationship with the Lord. They can, with the wisdom of God and keen spiritual discernment on your part, come out from their small world of Self and into being centered in God. Your tools are love and patience--prayer and scripture. Read to them the Word of God. God's Word has the power within it to accomplish what God sent it to do. Try recorded scripture, tapes and hymns or sacred music on CD or tape. Sing or hum to yourself as you feed, pour water, help to the bath room during the care-taking. If you play a musical instrument, take it and play praises to God. Start reading favorite accounts of Old Testament exploits with sacred music in the background. Pray with them, pray over them whether they protest or not. There has to be a change in the spiritual atmosphere surrounding them. You are changing it by bringing God into focus. You can even use the old Hollywood movies of the Bible where favorite movie stars play Moses and David.

A child cannot resist a good story, so pick out books to read to him about Bible heroes. Talk about those godly principles that are prominent in the story. Just get God's Word into his ears and eyes in as many ways as possible. If he protests, politely excuse yourself, so that he gets the idea that you and God's Word go together. In other words, you control the visit and the relationship with the guidance from the Holy Spirit. If he wants you there, he is stuck with hearing the Word of the Lord. Let God's word do the work. Take his control of your attention and point him to God. There must be a spiritual atmosphere, a desire for God's presence, before God can work. Until God is called into the situation, changing the atmosphere, nothing will measurably improve.

Faith comes by hearing and hearing by the Word of God. You don't have to convince or persuade the Self-centered loved one of anything. God's Word and the Holy Spirit are well able to do that. You have to understand that you are doing nothing of your Self. God is the change agent. So recognize that the child will eventually see peace and Jesus in you and come to relate to you on God's terms, not his. Persist! Do not let the child control the relationship. A child's will is strong, but he recognizes love when he sees it in your eyes and your actions. You are offering him ripe, delicious fruits of the Spirit - gentleness, kindness, peace, joy, and love. How can he resist when these are the very things that he needs and unconsciously wants?

Speak to children and adults in Psalms and accounts of Jesus' ministry. Ignore protests, demands and manipulations, even insults and threats. They're going to do that anyway, no matter what you do. Decide from the beginning to be determined. Know in your heart that you are there because God sent you. If they don't want to hear about God from you, then they don't want you there either. Do not allow your feelings to be hurt or for them to make you feel guilty or angry. Keep your eyes upon Jesus. You are there to express God's love, not to re-enforce Self-*ish* Self-love. Be kind and gentle in expressing your love no matter what! Anything you do will not make a difference in attitude unless you know that you are there to serve God, not a tyrannical, hurting ego. Learn to discern the difference between demands of ego and genuine need. Ask God. He will guide you.

This can be an exciting journey for both you and the needy person. Under no circumstances are you to feel guilty to allow the Self-centered loved one to <u>make</u> you feel guilty. Guilt is not of God. This is a war of wills. God's will and Self will. God wins. Self will loses even if it appears to win. We all have freedom of choice given to us by God. If someone insists on being Self-centered, God will honor his choice and allow him to be so. It is not within your ability to change <u>anyone</u>. God can change the loved one – but won't for He has given everyone the right to choose. It has to be the individual's choice.

2. CONNECT WITH THE HOLY SPIRIT IN PRAYER

Pray first for wisdom and patience for your Self, and then for others who have allowed Self-centeredness to control their lives.

Prayer for my SELF:
O Lord, My God, You know what I need and will supply those things, but I'm always bugging You with things that I think I need. I have even accused You for not loving me when You don't answer my self-ish prayers immediately. I confess at times I have not sought You in prayer because I love You, but because I need or want something that, in my judgment,

would give me pleasure or make me feel better. I have not thought of You as a person who loves me and has emotions and feelings, too.

Your Word says that You want me to love You or why else would You give me the first commandment: "You shall have no other gods before me."? **Exodus 20:4.** *You want my exclusive devotion, for You are a jealous God. You will not put up with my double-mindedness. I must worship You as my God without rivalry from any source, especially Self.*

In **Exodus 20:6** *You have said, "but showing love to a thousand generations of those who love me and keep my commandments". Teach me to love You* <u>intensely</u>, <u>passionately</u>, *God. I want to know* <u>You</u>. *I want to know Your ways. I want to keep Your commandments. I want to change and put You, not Self, FIRST in my life. I give up the idol of Self love. Thank You for calling me to be Your child. You are my Abba, Father, my ever-loving God. AMEN* (firm and established)

Prayer for OTHERS:
Father, I lift up this Self-centered person to You. You love him more than I do. I know that You desire a relationship with him. Teach me to bring Your powerful Word into his life so that he may choose to be Your child and place You on the throne of his heart. Anoint my words and prayers with Your power as I minister Your will to him. I fully expect for Your Word to change this person's life. I will be Your voice and Your hands, and Your example to serve to guide him into a personal relationship with You. I agree with You for Your purpose for his life. Lord, You are well able to do this, and I thank You for empowering me to execute Your will here, in this place, in this person, through Your love for him. AMEN (firm and established)

3. BREAK THE ROCK OF SELF-CENTEREDNESS WITH THE HAMMER OF GOD'S WORD.

Explore what is God's part and <u>underline</u> it then explore your part and (circle) it. Select at least one verse to memorize and recall when you recognize that you are falling back into the old habit of Self-focus. Select a scripture, one that you find especially meaningful for you. Write it on a card. Post it. Memorize it.

1 John 3 *Dear children, let us not love with words or tongue, but with actions and in truth.*

1 John 3:21 *...If our hearts do not condemn us we have confidence before God and receive from Him anything we ask because we obey His commands and do what pleases Him.*

2 John 6 *And this is love: that we walk in obedience to His commands. As you have heard from the beginning, His command is that you walk in love.*

John 5:44 *How can you believe if you accept praise from one another; yet make no effort to obtain the praise that comes from God only?*

***1John 3:17 *If anyone has material possessions and sees his brother in need, but has no pity on him, how can the love of God be in him?*

John 15:5 *I am the vine, you are the branches: he that abides in me, and I in him, the same brings forth much fruit: for without Me you can do nothing.* You cannot bring forth fruit from your Self. You must live in relationship with God and Jesus, His Son.

See also **John 14:15, John 15:12, Luke 7:42, Luke 10:27, Luke 16:13.**

DECLARE: **I am now centered in God, Who is my source of strength and salvation. Anyone that God calls for me to minister to, who is Self-centered, I declare that I will faithfully read, or in some spoken or visual way get God's Word to their ears and eyes. This is the spiritual support that they need. The healing power of the Holy Spirit is in God's Word. In ministering to someone who is Self-centered, I can see my own tendencies to act similarly. When I minister and care for a Self- centered loved one, I lose my Self and am centered in God. God has loved me with an everlasting love and has drawn me to Himself with His loving kindness. I want to live in Him. I will seek His face and learn His ways. I desire to love Him with all my heart and strength and mind and to love my neighbor (particularly any Self-centered neighbor) as my Self. I have the Holy Spirit power in me to help me fulfill these desires. I leave behind anything in my life that shows evidence of Self-centeredness. I reach forward to my goal of honoring and knowing my God who** rules and reigns above all powers and all created things. I have broken the rock of Self-centeredness with the hammer of God's Word. I declare that my mind is renewed to focus on Jesus. In Him I live and move and have my being. Let this always be true in my life.

Congratulations!
You have accomplished much.

You have lifted the heavy burdens of Self and placed them far from you on the shelf. They no longer keep you apart from God. You are free to walk in close proximity with God, that is-- getting as near as you can get to God without allowing your Self in between. It was a difficult journey.

Now you must decide if you want to go farther – to hear answers without questioning: "Is this You, my God whom I am hearing, or is it my deceptive heart or maybe even the enemy planting lovely, tempting lies in my thoughts?" Do you want to recognize God's voice without doubt? The prophets did not doubt when they heard God speaking to them. They knew His voice. You, too, can learn to know God's voice with the help of the Holy Spirit. He will teach you how to recognize and illuminate God's voice in a way unique to you which clearly separates His voice from deceptive voices.

There is always more in God. He places no limits upon you. It is important to keep your adventure with God going and growing to avoid becoming comfortable, satisfied, and content. As in all living things of this world, once you stop growing, you start to rot. Be ever renewed in your relationship with God like a tree that is planted by the river of waters. Your leaf will not wither and whatever you do will prosper.

WORDS OF ENCOURAGEMENT AND CAUTION
FOR YOUR CONTINUED JOURNEY

STAY ALERT ! BE ON GUARD!
KEEP SEEKING NEW THINGS IN GOD!

You will be tested! Your Self will try to regain the control you have given to the Holy Spirit. Habit, comfort, and Self-deception are its weapons. It is easy to slip back if you are not watching Once you have put your Self high on the shelf, do not return it to its former place of control. That makes you unstable as the waves of the ocean. You have a renewed mind. You are free of the domination of Self in the areas you have hammered into pieces with God's Word. Stay free. Be vigilant.

Be mindful that there are several more areas controlled by Self which you have yet to challenge and place under the control of the Holy Spirit. Continue to draw near to God and He will draw near to you. There are no limitations on closeness. You can get close enough to God where mere whispers can be as thunderclaps. You can lean your head upon His breast and listen to the rumble of God's mountain-moving voice. Do you want to get your answers in intimacy, spirit to spirit or are you content with long distance? You can be in His presence and talk with Him about anything and everything at any time. Think about it. All it costs is giving the Holy Spirit control of more Self areas of your life. Learn to feed your spirit and starve your Self. Become strong in the Lord and mighty by His power.

Put Your Self on the Shelf - Book 2 can help you deal with several of the toughest Self areas to place in God's control: Self defense, Self help, and Self-support and Self-image. All of these things you have been taught by the world to do without God's help. Compare *your* track record in those areas with God's unfailing promises recorded in His word. It's a no-brainer!

I pray God's rich blessings on you for your continued journey. Be single-minded. Keep your eyes upon Jesus. Thank God for what He has already done in your life then--continue your journey to awesome prayer power fired with the truth of God's Word.

Marion Clark, Intercessor

NOTE: Put Your Self On The Self Book 1 individual or small group manual of practical application may be downloaded free of charge at www.singingharp.com.

Additional copies of Book 1 are also available for purchase at this website.

TEACHING TALES
BY
AUNTIE M

(A subsidiary ministry of Marion Clark)

Auntie M ministry teaches both Christian principles and facts about science and the world through picture books. It is directed towards pre-school children through primary grades.

THE BASIC FOCUS of this ministry is to teach children how to trust God, to know that He always loves them, and that He protects them. Safety and nurturing are their basic needs. I have long felt that many Christian children are not being taught enough to have faith in God either by example in the family or by experiences and the teachings of a traditional church.

If children don't learn to love and trust God at an early age, before the world gets to them with fear and criticism, then they will have a hard time trusting Him and desiring a personal relationship with Him as an adult. Picture stories work.

I teach basic Christian principles. Having spent 32 years in the public school system I know the value of teaching a strong foundation upon which to build faith or any other essential concept whether spiritual or educational. If you don't have the basics, how can anything more complex make sense?

Children's picture books are available at www.singingharp.com.

The following are some of the <u>picture book titles</u> available now or within the next year at <u>www.singingharp.com</u>.

The title, <u>Billy Bulb's Great Adventure</u> was suggested by the author of <u>Peter Pan</u>, James M. Barrie who said, "To die will be an awfully big adventure." This picture book is two stories in one of how things naturally die, but in doing so they change. Also on a spiritual level it explains of how the "tickle-Ickle" flower bud, which is a person's spirit, changes into something new, both beautiful and eternal. The science lesson of the life cycle of a flower bulb is a tool for teaching children about death and resurrection. The book is spiral bound and printed on heavy paper for little hands.

<u>Fly Li'l Eagle, Fly</u> is a picture book journey from fear to faith. It is told as a parable about a little eagle that falls out of a lofty nest. He is rescued and cared for by a man wise in the ways of God's creatures. The man represents the loving care of God and the little eagle represents a small child that he loves and cares for. Many facts about eagles are woven throughout the story of how this little helpless eaglet grows to become the King of Birds soaring effortlessly in the heavens. Through faith and trust in God all things are possible.

<u>Heaven's Gonna' Be Boring</u> ---- A busy, active boy wants nothing to do with heaven because he thinks only old people go there and he won't get to play baseball anymore. It is a way of explaining things about heaven that adults don't normally have time to research or even think about themselves. How can you be prepared to tell a child something about heaven when the question comes out of the blue? The story is told in a noisy family setting when Andy says, "I do-wanna go to heaven. It's gonna be boring!"

<u>Little Boy, Little Boy</u> ---- The story is told in folk tale fashion with the quest and discovery format of three. The Little Boy repeats the phrase, "This I must know. Where does love come from and where does it go?" He finds out. He finds God.

<u>God Doesn't do Magic!</u> ---- This picture tale comes in rhyme with a Gardenin' Angel who speaks like he's from the Bronx. His job is to watch over twins that get into magic stuff and actually try it out in disobedience to their parents. The purpose of the story is to emphasize obedience to your parents and to counteract the cuteness of magic like funny witches and Casper the friendly ghost without making it scary. The guardenin' (guardian) angel is a cookie-eating heel-clicking, loving character.

<u>Abigail's Big Question</u> ---- A energetic little girl wants to talk to God but doesn't know how. It helps parents to teach their children to pray – really! No wrote prayers to a big somebody in the sky. It teaches that God is near and you can <u>really</u> talk to Him.

SINGING HARP MINISTRY

The history of the harp goes back to 3000BC in the Book of Genesis of the Bible. Jubal is mentioned in Genesis 4:21 as the father of all the harp players. The psaltery and the lyre are both forms of the harp, strings across an open framework. Harps were used by prophets when they gave a Word from God to the people. David, both as a shepherd and as king of Israel, constructed harps and played them as he worshipped the Lord God. Solomon imported special wood for the making of harps for worship in the temple. Harps were played day and night without ceasing in the temple as praise and an offering to God.

Why was the harp in such prominence in Bible history? It has a power that no other instrument possesses when played in faith. David played the harp for Saul to rout a demon. Harps were commonly used in healing. The Spiritual power of the harp was a part of cleansing the temple in the time of Hezekiah and then prominent again in the dedication of Solomon's temple. No other instrument recorded in the Bible has such power in worship and healing.

Today harps are used to promote healing in hospitals. The healing quality of musical instruments is now a recognized therapy in many states with the licensing of musicians trained in healing with music. By chance I watched a television program which reported how nurses assigned to premature babies were amazed that the babies noticeably thrived when a harp was played in the hospital nursery. When the music was recorded and played in the absence of the harpist, there was no positive change in the progress of the babies. Maybe this was not a scientific study, but worth investigation don't you think?

I play a Celtic folk harp named Praise (It is traditional to name your harp.) The music of the harp leads people into the throne room of God. It helps them to connect with God through worship. Even those who don't know God experience great peace at the sound of the harp. It is a combination of sound vibrations and faith that attracted me to the harp. I held it in awe. When an opportunity came for me to own a small folk harp I did not hesitate to purchase it. I set it in a corner for 2 years just looking at it, afraid to even attempt to play it. When I worked up the courage and decided to actually learn to play the harp, I could not find a teacher. That was a good thing! If I had classical training I would have been trained as a performer, not a worshiper. I did not want to strive for excellence in executing the music but to praise God with my harp. For me, praise could not be done when tied to reading notes as written. It was when I abandoned the restriction of the notated music that I learned to play from my heart and my spirit. With that decision, the Singing Harp Ministry was born. God used my faith to connect with my fingers, bypassing my brain, feeding my spirit. This led to ministering in prayer retreats and prayer workshops. The following are some of the fruits of that decision:

1. <u>Accompanying</u> the speaking of God's Words of edification with the harp. Speaking the Psalms and playing the harp as David did while he tended the sheep, is a great joy and a blessing to me.

2. <u>Praying and interceding</u> through the music of the harp. The act of creating a musical prayer connects me with the Holy Spirit. He continues to teach me to pray and directs my fingers in prayer.

3. <u>Meditating on scripture</u> through the harp. I just take a scripture written on my heart and begin to wonder and wander letting the Holy Spirit lead me into new places, new revelations.

4. <u>Warring with the harp.</u> At times I have been called to War with the harp. This is a time initiated only by the Holy Spirit when the music changes without my realizing it. The fingers and notes leave a worship mode becoming almost strident. Wherever God leads, my fingers follow creating the music of worship or war according to His will.

Marion Clark, Intercessor

More information is available at the
website www.singingharp.com.